I0820324

SWEET SAFFRON AND CARDAMOM

SWEET SAFFRON AND CARDAMOM

SPICED DESSERTS FROM AN IMMIGRANT KITCHEN

Ashia Ismail-Singer

Photography by Christall Lowe

INTERLINK BOOKS
AN IMPRINT OF INTERLINK PUBLISHING GROUP, INC.
NORTHAMPTON, MASSACHUSETTS

Contents

Introduction

Every since publishing my first cookbook, *Ashia's Indian Kitchen*, I have been itching to get into a book full of sweetness with a touch of spice. Using spices in sweets and desserts has been done for centuries in the East; some of the common spices used for this purpose are saffron, cardamom, cinnamon, star anise and nutmeg.

I grew up learning to balance spices in my cooking, and so the concept of incorporating spices into some of the sweets and desserts I make regularly seemed like an inspired idea. It's probably not surprising then that this book shares recipes that combine sweet with spices; a flavor match made in heaven.

My recipes tell a story, my story, one that I love sharing. Of Indian heritage, I was born and brought up in Malawi, Africa. My grandparents, both Muslim, moved there from the Gujarat, India, in the late 1940s, around the time of the partition between India and Pakistan.

In the late 1980s, political instability in Malawi caused my family to move to the United Kingdom in search of a better life and education. After having grown up in a different way of life, living in the UK was quite a shock to the system. At home in Malawi, we had a cook, a gardener and a nanny. We had chickens and goats, we grew our own vegetables and what we didn't grow, we bought directly from the people who would come door-to-door selling their vegetables from the back of their bikes. Life was very different.

After leaving school in the UK, I went to art college where I studied fashion and design, but after two years I felt something was lacking. At this point I decided I wanted to be able to travel with my career and to help people, so I chose to study nursing.

Although my family was with me in the UK, I never really felt I belonged there. I sensed an undercurrent of racism that didn't sit well with me and so I traveled to the USA, hoping to work as a nurse there and maybe find somewhere I could truly call home. But when things didn't work out as planned, a good friend suggested I go to New Zealand; he had spent time there and felt sure I would love it. And so I moved to New Zealand in early 1997, where soon after my arrival in this amazing country, I met my Kiwi husband of 27 years.

I first started writing this book during a very unsettling time in the world, during the lockdown resulting from the Covid-19 pandemic that has caused havoc to the health and economy of the world. Being housebound gave me time to reflect about the way we talk to people and share stories and recipes. Now more than ever, I feel there's a need for cookbooks, recipes and food stories to help us through trying times.

Nothing gives me more pleasure than baking and sharing. Anyone who knows me will tell you that. I get it from my mom, who is always cooking for others—it makes her feel she's making a difference. I love whipping up a batch of muffins to give to a friend, baking a cake for a birthday celebration, baking goodies to give as gifts—the list goes on.

What's better than curling up on the sofa with a cup of something hot and a slice of something sweet? The aromas of cinnamon and nutmeg in your hot chocolate and the comforting smell of cardamom in your bread pudding. In *Sweet Saffron and Cardamom* you will find recipes to suit all your baking needs, from comfort baking to more elaborate treats. And all with a hint of spice to balance the sweetness. Sugar, which features in this book, has long been the "enemy" in today's ever-changing fad diets and fashionable foods. But I firmly believe that once in a while we all need a treat, something sweet to satisfy our cravings and celebrate those special moments in life—let's just be careful not to overdo it. It's also worth noting that everything I use in this book, sugar and other ingredients, is there for everyone to see—nothing is hidden, what you see is what you get.

This book is organized into seasonal chapters and in many cases, the recipes feature seasonal fruits that I pair with complementary spices. There's ginger, cardamom and star anise in fall desserts baked with apples and pears. Cinnamon, vanilla and saffron are paired with summer berries and stone fruits to make luscious desserts, ice creams and cakes. There are also gluten- and dairy-free options throughout. My intention is that this book will take you through the year, giving you pleasure whatever the weather.

Overall, the recipes—including some traditional English, American, and New Zealander ones to which I've given an Eastern twist—are easy to make and may even revive a few of your old favorites. I do hope you enjoy baking and sharing them as much as I enjoy sharing them.

Much love,

Ashia

Baking with spices

I have my favorite spices that I use in baking and desserts: saffron, cardamom, star anise, cinnamon, to name a few. While the recipes in this book are designed to be simple, the addition of a spice or two will give your desserts and cakes a subtle yet complex flavor profile. For me, baking with spices comes naturally as I have always done it, but those unfamiliar with using spice in baking will find these subtly exotic flavors to be a real taste sensation as well as taking your baking to the next level. What's more, the ingredients are widely available, making the recipes perfectly doable for any home baker.

STORING SPICES

The spices featured in this book are readily available in supermarkets or specialty stores. They need to be fresh so it's best to buy small quantities at a time and store them in small glass jars with airtight lids.

PREPARATION OF SPICES

Powdered spices are convenient and easy. If spices need grinding, use a spice grinder, a coffee grinder or crush them with a mortar and pestle. I also use a microplane or zester for some spices.

Spices and other ingredients used in this book

BASIL
Not a spice but a herb that is great in baking, and particularly good with strawberries and for infusing sugar. Depending on the variety you use, it can add a clove flavor or citrus notes in the case of lemon basil. Toss the leaves through a fruit salad or use them in your homemade syrups.

BASIL SEEDS
Very similar to chia seeds, basil seeds swell in liquid. Full of nutritional properties such as fiber, iron and calcium, they are traditionally used in Ayurvedic and Chinese medicine. In the East they are used in milky drinks, ice creams, smoothies, yogurts and puddings.

BLACK PEPPER
One of the most frequently used spices, black pepper has a pungent flavor and aroma—a mixture of heat and citrus, plus earthy, smoky and floral notes. It's best to buy whole peppercorns and grind them as required.

CARDAMOM
Green cardamom, one of my favorite spices to use in baking, has a floral sweetness that is great in both sweet and savory cooking. The outer shell is crushed to release small brown seeds, which can also be crushed or left whole. You can use both the seeds and the whole cardamom pod to flavor your baking and desserts.

CINNAMON
Another one of my favorite spices to use, cinnamon comes in the form of a ground spice and sticks or quills. There are two types: cassia and true cinnamon. The more popular one to use in desserts and baking is true cinnamon as it has a fragrant, sweet and aromatic flavor.

CHILE
Many of us already add this to savory dishes, but used in small amounts it works remarkably well in chocolate-based desserts.

CLOVES
Available whole or powdered, this will add a spicy, woody flavor to desserts, but do be careful not to over-use—you don't want to overpower your dish.

FENNEL
Adds a sweet licorice flavor to drinks and ice cream.

FIVE SPICE
This Chinese blend of warm and complex spices—typically star anise, cloves, cinnamon, Szechuan peppercorns, and fennel seeds—is great in cakes, cookies and hot drinks. I also add ginger. You can blend your own using a mortar and pestle.

GINGER
Fresh ginger and ground ginger work really well in both sweet and savory dishes and hot and cold drinks. Its fresh yet spicy taste also works really well in desserts and cakes and while dried ground ginger doesn't have the same intensity as fresh, it adds a richness and spiciness that works very well with sweet dishes.

LAVENDER

Food-grade lavender (which can be bought in specialty stores) is best to use in cooking and baking. Like vanilla, a little goes a long way. Part of the mint family, lavender flowers are often used in baking, giving a lovely scent that is fruity and floral—and sometimes woody and earthy, depending on the variety. You can also infuse it in sugar or use it to decorate your cakes and cookies.

MINT

A lovely refreshing herb that pairs well with chocolate, ice cream and cookies, leaving a cool, fresh aftertaste. It is known to have benefits for anxiety and upset tummies.

NUTMEG

Pungent, warm and slightly sharp, this strong spice is best stored whole and then grated when required.

ORANGE BLOSSOM WATER

A distilled water containing essential oils from orange blossoms. It is frequently used in Persian and Arabic cooking. It adds a fragrant citrus flavor to desserts and is best used sparingly.

PINK PEPPERCORNS

These come from a different plant than black or white peppercorns. When crushed they give an aroma similar to black peppercorns and have a warm, bright and astringent flavor. Great for cookies.

POPPY SEEDS

Sourced from the poppy flower, there are two types of seeds: the white ones have a sweet aroma and nutty flavor while the dark-blue version is nutty and fruity. Perfect for toppings on breads, cakes and cookies.

ROSE PETALS (DRIED)

It's best to use the food-grade variety, which has many uses including decoration or as an addition to your tea. They have a distinctive sweet floral and musky aroma—and they look so pretty.

ROSE WATER

Similar to orange blossom water, rose water adds a fresh floral flavor to desserts. It works well with spices like saffron and cardamom and with nuts like pistachio and almond. Rose water brings out the sweetness in a recipe and balances more tart ingredients.

SAFFRON

Another stunning spice that can be used in both sweet and savory dishes, this is one of the most expensive spices and has many flavor profiles: earthy and bittersweet with a sweet, hay-like aroma. Iranian, Kashmiri and Spanish saffron is the best quality.

STAR ANISE

A very pretty, elegant-looking spice with an aniseedy flavor. Used whole, it adds a wonderful warming flavor to fruits in desserts. It's one of the key ingredients in Chinese five spice.

TURMERIC

Fresh turmeric is sweet, mild and aromatic, while dried turmeric is slightly bitter. It's the key ingredient in my turmeric latte as it has many health benefits, including anti-inflammatory properties.

VANILLA

Vanilla beans are best when you want intense flavor. However, vanilla paste and extract is readily available and the extract, which is okay to use for baking, is probably the cheapest alternative.

“Summer has filled her veins with light and her heart is washed with noon . . .”

C. DAY LEWIS

Summer

The sweetness of summer blooms from the briskness of spring, bringing to our kitchens glossy plums, luscious peaches and tangy berries mixed with spices to itensify tarts and cakes. Add a hint of chai spices to a popsicle to cool you down on a hot day. Whisk up a bowl of hot cherry fritters dusted with cinnamon sugar to share with friends al fresco. Simple recipes like these will take you through the hottest season, using spices to turn your summer fruits into luscious desserts and baking worth sharing.

I first made this when we were living in England and had some stale brioche loaf left over. I decided to make it into a brioche pudding. My family was living nearby and so often came over for impromptu dinners—they loved sampling my recipes. This one is a great crowd-pleaser and so quick and easy to make.

Spiced brioche berry pudding

SERVES 6–8

1 brioche loaf

10½ oz (300 g) raspberries (fresh is best)

7 oz (200 g) white chocolate, coarsely chopped

3 eggs

1 teaspoon vanilla bean paste or extract

½ teaspoon ground cinnamon

pinch of ground cardamom

2⅓ cups (550 ml) sour cream

confectioners' sugar or grated white chocolate to decorate

ice cream or whipped cream to serve

Preheat the oven to 425°F (220°C).

Cut the loaf into slices and then into ¾–1 in (2–3 cm) squares. Put half of the squares into a 10 in (25 cm) baking dish. Sprinkle half of the raspberries on top, followed by half of the chocolate. Repeat with the remaining bread, raspberries and chocolate.

Make a custard by beating the eggs, vanilla, spices and sour cream together, preferably using a hand mixer or a wooden spoon. Pour the custard over the bread mixture.

Bake for about 30 minutes or until golden.

Remove from the oven and leave to stand for 10 minutes to allow the custard to set. Sprinkle with confectioners' sugar or grated white chocolate and serve with ice cream or fresh whipped cream.

Serving these baked plums with a sweet puri adds a crunchy dimension, but you can also serve them with whipped cream or ice cream.

Cinnamon plums with sweet puri

SERVES 4–6

CINNAMON PLUMS

8 plums (or any stone fruit), halved and pitted

2 tablespoons brown sugar

½ teaspoon ground cinnamon

2 tablespoons butter

mascarpone, to serve

SWEET PURI

1 cup (125 g) all-purpose flour, sifted

¼ teaspoon baking powder

¼ teaspoon salt

1 teaspoon sugar

1 tablespoon vegetable oil

extra oil to shallow fry

Preheat the oven to 425°F (220°C).

First, make the plums: In a shallow dish (a gratin dish would work well), arrange the fruit in a tight-fitting single layer. Mix together the sugar and cinnamon and sprinkle over the plums. Dot butter around the fruit. Bake for 20–25 minutes until tender and golden.

To make the sweet puri, mix all of the ingredients, except for the oil for shallow frying. Gradually mix in up to ½ cup (120 ml) of water to make a soft dough.

Divide the dough into 10–12 pieces. Roll each piece into a ball then, using a rolling pin, roll each ball out to form 3–4 in (8–10 cm) circles.

Add enough oil to a small deep pan to come about a third of the way up the sides. Heat the oil to a temperature of about 350°F (180°C) and fry the puri in small batches, spooning hot oil over to make them puff up. Once cooked, remove them with a slotted spoon and place on paper towels to absorb excess oil.

Serve hot, with the baked fruit and a dollop of mascarpone.

Sharbat is the name for a sweet drink usually made from fruit and flowers. I make triple batches of this concentrated syrup at a time—so it's ready to be mixed with soda or iced water at a moment's notice. It'll keep in the fridge for up to a week.

Lime, ginger & mint sharbat

MAKES ABOUT 2½ CUPS (600 ML)

1½ cups (300 g) sugar

1½ cups (350 ml) boiling water

2 cardamom pods, slightly crushed

¾ oz (20 g) fresh ginger root, coarsely chopped

zest of 2 limes

½ cup (120–130 ml) freshly squeezed lime juice

small handful of mint leaves, finely chopped, plus extra to serve

soda water or still water to serve

In a heatproof pitcher, dissolve the sugar in the boiling water.

Add the cardamom and the ginger and leave to cool. Once cooled, pick out the cardamom pods and discard, and then transfer the liquid to a blender. Add the lime juice and blend until smooth.

Pass the mixture through a sieve, then stir in the lime zest and mint. Refrigerate until needed.

Serve with ice, soda water and a sprig of mint.

This is a divine way to cool down in the summer. If you can't source fresh mangoes, use canned, puréed or even frozen mango (all available in South Asian grocery stores). The popsicles are such a delicious cold and tropical treat, particularly after a barbecue on a hot summer's day. Leave the cayenne pepper out of the dipping sugar for a more child-friendly option.

Mango popsicles with coconut dipping sugar

MAKES 8

2 cups (400 g) puréed mango (about 6 fresh mangoes)
1 cup (240 g) coconut milk
pinch of cinnamon
2–3 cardamom pods, crushed and seeds reserved
8 popsicle sticks

DIPPING SUGAR

1 tablespoon coarse brown sugar
1 tablespoon white sugar
1 tablespoon sea salt
1 tablespoon desiccated coconut
pinch of cayenne pepper (optional)

Using a handheld immersion blender, mix the puréed mango with the coconut milk. Add the spices and mix again. Pour the mixture into eight popsicle molds or large ice-cube trays and freeze for 6–8 hours (overnight is best). When the mixture is semi-frozen (40–60 minutes), insert a popsicle stick in each.

Just before serving, mix together the ingredients for the dipping sugar. Sprinkle some on each popsicle, or your family and guests can help themselves.

This beautifully moist chai-flavored loaf featured in my first cookbook. I'm including it here, but this time I'm using blueberries instead of raspberries. However, any berries would work really well—the result will be a delectable loaf with a vibrant berry frosting that has just the right amount of sweetness and tang.

Frosted blueberry & chai loaf

SERVES 10

⅔ cup (150 ml) milk
2 chai-flavored tea bags
2 eggs
1 cup (200 g) sugar (preferably superfine)
½ teaspoon vanilla extract or vanilla bean paste
⅔ cup (200 g) all-purpose flour
1 teaspoon baking powder
1 teaspoon ground cinnamon
⅓ cup (80 ml) vegetable oil
¾ cup (120 g) blueberries (fresh or frozen)

ICING

2 cups (227 g) confectioners' sugar, sifted
¼ cup (40 g) fresh or thawed blueberries
¼ cup (40 g) fresh blueberries to garnish

Preheat the oven to 325°F (170°C). Grease and line a 9½ x 5 in (24 x 12 cm) loaf pan.

In a small saucepan, bring the milk to a boil and add the tea bags. Stir, then set aside to cool, leaving the tea bags in the milk.

Using an electric mixer, beat the eggs, sugar and vanilla together until thick and glossy. Sift in the flour, baking powder and cinnamon. Add the oil and a scant ½ cup (100 ml) of the milk/tea mixture (note that you will have to squeeze the tea bags to make the mixture up to a scant ½ cup (100 ml), as some of the milk will have evaporated), then mix at a slow speed just until fully combined, taking care not to over-mix.

In a separate bowl, crush the berries with a fork, retaining some of the shape. Do not drain as the juice will be laced through the cake. Gently fold the semi-crushed berries through the cake mixture.

Pour the mixture into the prepared loaf pan and bake for 45 minutes or until a skewer inserted into the center comes out clean. Once cool, turn out of the pan.

To make the icing, process the confectioners' sugar and fresh or thawed berries in a blender until they reach a thick, spreadable consistency. Using a knife, spread the icing over the loaf and decorate with the fresh blueberries.

The Arabic word halva translates to "sweetness"and can be made with a variety of ingredients that produce different textures from grainy to silky smooth. Very similar to Italian panna cotta, you can flavor it with anything you like—I've used cardamom and orange blossom water here.

Cardamom & orange halva

SERVES 6

1¼ cups (300 ml) heavy cream

2 cups (500 ml) whole milk

¼ cup (50 g) sugar

1 teaspoon agar agar mixed with 1 tablespoon water*

2 teaspoons semolina

1 teaspoon orange blossom water

3–4 cardamom pods, slightly crushed

cotton candy to garnish**

Using a handheld mixer, whisk the cream and milk together, then pour the mixture into a pot and add the sugar. Bring to a boil for just 1 minute.

Reduce the heat and then add the agar agar mixture, semolina, orange blossom water and cardamom pods. Simmer for 6–8 minutes.

Pick out the cardamom pods and then pour into a shallow dish or your preferred molds/dessert glasses and allow to cool. Refrigerate until set, 2–3 hours. If using molds, remove the halva by running a knife around the edges. Decorate with cotton candy.

* Agar agar, which I use in preference to gelatin, can be bought from Asian grocery stores and most supermarkets. Made out of seaweed, it is a vegetarian setting agent and comes in powder form.

** Arabic or Turkish Cotton candy can be bought from specialty food stores.

Galettes are so easy to make. For me, fresh berry pies and easy baked desserts are best eaten outside on a summer evening with loved ones.

Blackberry, lime & cinnamon galettes

SERVES 6–8

- **14 oz (400 g) puff pastry, thawed**
- **⅓ cup (30 g) ground almonds**
- **13 oz (375 g) fresh blackberries**
- **1 teaspoon finely grated lime zest**
- **⅓ cup (70 g) sugar (preferably superfine)**
- **2 teaspoons cornstarch**
- **1 teaspoon finely chopped mint**
- **1½–2 tablespoons butter, cut into small pieces**
- **1 egg, lightly beaten**
- **½ teaspoon ground cinnamon**
- **2 tablespoons raw sugar**
- **mint sprigs to decorate**
- **whipped cream or ice cream to serve**

Preheat the oven to 400°F (200°C).

Roll out the pastry between two sheets of parchment paper to form a 14 in (35 cm) circle about ⅛ in (4 mm) thick. Carefully transfer the pastry to a large baking sheet and remove the top sheet of parchment paper.

Spread the pastry with ground almonds, leaving a 1½–2 in (4–5 cm) border around the outside.

In a bowl combine the blackberries, lime zest, sugar, cornstarch and mint and toss. Gently top the ground almonds with this mixture, and then scatter the butter over the top.

Fold the border of the pastry in toward the center, pressing the edges together gently to close; this will look quite rustic, which is the beauty of this easy dessert. Brush the top with the beaten egg.

Mix the cinnamon and raw sugar and sprinkle all over the galette and pastry.

Bake at 400°F (200°C) for 10 minutes, then reduce the heat to 350°F (180°C) for 30–40 minutes or until pastry looks golden and the fruit is bubbling.

Allow to cool before decorating with mint. Serve with whipped cream or ice cream.

This is an easy, no-bake cheesecake. The passion fruit provides a sharp, tangy flavor that cuts through the creaminess of the dessert beautifully. You can replace the passion fruit with berries if you prefer. I have leftovers for breakfast the next day. I dare you not to!

Passion fruit & ginger cheesecake

SERVES 8–10

BASE

14 oz (400 g) ginger cookies

8 tablespoons (120 g) butter

FILLING

1 cup (250 g) mascarpone

⅔ cup (75 g) confectioners' sugar

1 teaspoon vanilla extract or 1 vanilla bean, seeds scraped

1⅔ cups (400 ml) crème fraîche

1¼ cups (300 ml) heavy cream

4–5 ripe passion fruit*

Crush the cookies into fine crumbs. In a saucepan, melt the butter and stir in the crumbs. Tip the mixture into a 9 in (22 cm) springform cake pan and press down. Refrigerate until firm, 45 minutes to 1 hour, or in the freezer if you are in a hurry.

Beat the mascarpone and confectioners' sugar in an electric mixer until smooth. Stir in the vanilla and crème fraîche.

In a separate bowl, whip the cream until it stands in soft peaks (take care not to overwhip), then gently fold it into the mascarpone mixture. Scrape the mixture onto the cookie base, cover with plastic wrap and refrigerate for at least 3 hours to set.

To serve, remove the cake from the pan. Squeeze the passion fruit seeds and juice over the top and cut into portions to serve.

* Alternatively, replace the passion fruit with 10½ oz (300 g) mixed berries of your choice (blueberries and raspberries work well). In a saucepan, heat a pat of butter, then add ½ teaspoon vanilla and 2 tablespoons sugar. Gently stir in the berries and cook for 3–4 minutes until soft. Set aside to cool before spooning over the cheesecake.

Called falooda in some parts of India, these great summer coolers look so pretty when served in tall glasses. They are often drunk after breaking a fast during Ramadan.

Rose milkshakes

SERVES 4–6, DEPENDING ON THE SIZE OF THE GLASSES

ROSE SYRUP

1 cup (200 g) sugar

2 teaspoons rose water

pink food coloring

FALOODA

2 teaspoons agar agar*

1 cup (240 ml) boiling water

yellow food coloring

1 oz (30 g) basil seeds**

1 tablespoon confectioners' sugar

4 cups (950 ml) chilled milk

4–6 tablespoons thick whipped cream or ice cream

nuts, edible dried rose petals and mint leaves to garnish (optional)

To make the rose syrup, combine the sugar and 1 cup (240 ml) of water in a saucepan and bring to a boil. Boil for 2 minutes, then add the rose water and enough food coloring to make a pink syrup. Set aside to cool.

To make the falooda, place the agar agar in a small saucepan with the boiling water. Stir to dissolve, then cook over medium heat, stirring constantly, for 10–12 minutes. Add a little yellow food coloring, then pour into a large shallow dish and refrigerate until set. Turn out onto a board and cut into thin strips.

Soak the basil seeds in ⅓ cup (80 ml) of water for about 10 minutes. Stir the confectioners' sugar into the milk.

To serve, pour 2 tablespoons of rose syrup into each of the required number of tall glasses. Add some yellow falooda strips and about 2 teaspoons of basil seeds to each glass. Top with the sweetened chilled milk and a dollop of whipped cream or ice cream. Garnish with nuts, dried rose petals and mint leaves if desired.

* Agar agar, which I use in preference to gelatin, can be bought from Asian grocery stores and most supermarkets. Made out of seaweed, it is a vegetarian setting agent and comes in powder form.

**Available from Indian grocery stores.

I adore cherries, they are my favorite summer fruit. The season is so short that I make the most of it every year. This recipe will wow your family and friends and is best eaten hot with cardamom and cinnamon sugar, served with a cream of your choice.

Cherry fritters

SERVES 4–6

10½ oz (300 g) cherries, including the stems
⅓ cup (80 ml) milk
1 tablespoon melted butter
2 eggs, separated
½ cup (120 g) flour, sifted
½ cup (100 g) sugar (preferably superfine), plus 1 tablespoon
oil for frying
2 teaspoons ground cinnamon
¼ teaspoon ground cardamom
mascarpone to serve (optional)

Rinse and thoroughly dry the cherries. Whisk the milk, butter, egg yolks, flour and 1 tablespoon of sugar to make a smooth batter. In a separate bowl, beat the egg whites until soft peaks form, then fold them into the batter.

In a wok or small pot, heat a 2½ in (6 cm) depth of oil. It will be hot enough when a piece of bread carefully dipped into it quickly turns golden. Holding the cherries by their stalks, dip them in the batter, shaking off the excess, and then drop them into the hot oil. Fry until golden, about 1 minute, gently turning them after 30 seconds or so until they are evenly fried. Remove with a slotted spoon and drain on a paper towels.

Mix together spices and the remaining sugar and toss in the hot cherries to coat them. Serve immediately with mascarpone if desired.

The addition of pink peppercorns and Chinese five spice make these cookies a taste sensation. Any that are left over (they'll keep well in an airtight container for a week) are perfect with coffee.

Raspberry fool with spiced peppercorn cookies

SERVES 6–8

COOKIES

9 tablespoons (125 g) butter

¼ cup (50 g) sugar

¼ cup (50 g) brown sugar

¼ cup (60 ml) golden syrup (or light molasses)

2½ cups (300 g) all-purpose flour, plus extra for dusting

1 teaspoon baking soda

1 teaspoon ground ginger

2 teaspoons five spice powder

2 tablespoons pink peppercorns, coarsely crushed

RASPBERRY FOOL

9 oz (250 g) fresh raspberries, plus extra to serve

½ cup (100 g) sugar (preferably superfine)

finely grated zest and juice of 1 orange

1¼ cups (300 ml) heavy cream

¾ cup (200 g) crème fraîche

1 tablespoon confectioners' sugar

Preheat the oven to 350°F (180°C). Line a baking sheet with parchment paper.

In a large pot, melt the butter, sugars and golden syrup (or molasses), then set aside to cool slightly.

Sift the flour, baking soda, ginger and five spice into the pot. Stir until the mixture forms a stiff dough.

Turn the dough out onto a lightly floured surface and roll out very thinly (2 mm thick). Using a cookie cutter, cut the dough into your desired shapes and place on the lined pan. Sprinkle with the crushed peppercorns, lightly pressing them into the dough.

Bake until the cookies are crisp and golden, about 8 minutes. Remove from the oven and transfer to a wire rack to cool completely.

To make the fool, place the raspberries, sugar, orange juice and zest into a blender and purée. In a bowl or mixer, whisk the creams with the confectioners' sugar until you have soft peaks, taking care not to over-mix.

Swirl the purée through the cream mixture and spoon into glasses or small bowls. Refrigerate until ready to serve, topped with fresh raspberries and accompanied with the spiced cookies.

Refreshing and sweet with a hint of spice, these are perfect for a sizzling, hot day when you need to cool down. They also make an impressive after-dinner treat if you want to keep it simple. Don't be tempted to cut back on the sugar, since the pops will not taste as sweet after being frozen.

Chai masala popsicles with peanut & chocolate drizzle

MAKES 4

4–5 green cardamom pods, crushed and seeds reserved
4 whole cloves
¼ teaspoon fennel seeds
¼ teaspoon ground ginger
1 cinnamon stick (about finger length)
4 tablespoons sugar (or 2 tablespoons sweetened condensed milk)
1 tea bag
4 popsicle sticks

DRIZZLE

½ cup (85 g) chocolate chips or melts
¼ cup (70 g) crunchy peanut butter

In a pot, bring 2 cups (450 ml) water to a boil. Add the spices and the sugar (or condensed milk). Once it has dissolved, add the tea bag and simmer for a few minutes. Strain into a pitcher and leave to cool.

Stir the cooled mixture well, pour into popsicle molds and freeze. When the mixture is semi-frozen (after 40-60 minutes), insert a popsicle stick in each. Once frozen, remove from the molds by holding them under hot running water until they release.

To make the drizzle, heat the chocolate and peanut butter in short bursts in a microwave. Stir to mix and drizzle over the popsicles or simply dip the ends to make a chocolate tip. You may have to refreeze them to set the chocolate.

These moist little cakes make a delightful treat for afternoon tea. I've adapted the recipe from the one given to me by my lovely food stylist friend Bernadette (Bernie) Hogg, who I met on a magazine food shoot some years ago.

Blueberry & cinnamon friands

MAKES 9

6 egg whites
13 tablespoons (185 g) unsalted butter, melted
1½ cups (125 g) ground almonds
2 cups (240 g) confectioners' sugar, plus extra for dusting
⅔ cup (75 g) all-purpose flour
¼ teaspoon ground cinnamon
⅓ cup (50 g) fresh or frozen blueberries, other berries, or berry jam
whipped cream or Greek-style yogurt to serve

Preheat the oven to 350°F (180°C). Lightly grease a 9-hole oval friand pan with a little butter (if you don't have one, you can use 9 cups of a muffin pan).

In a medium bowl, lightly whisk the egg whites, then add the melted butter, ground almonds and confectioners' sugar. Using a wooden spoon, stir until just combined.

Sift the flour and cinnamon into a bowl, mix to combine, then gently fold into the egg mixture. Divide evenly among the cups in the prepared pan.

Place a cluster of berries (or a dollop of berry jam) on top of each friand.

Bake for 25 minutes or until the friands are light golden and spring back when pressed lightly with your finger. Remove from the oven and set aside for 5 minutes before transferring to a wire rack to cool completely.

Dust with confectioners' sugar and serve with yogurt or whipped cream.

I love no-churn ice creams; they are so simple to make. Even so, I have fond memories of handmade ice cream being churned by our cook back in Malawi. He used a wooden bucket with a metal cylinder in which the ingredients would be placed. Ice and salt would be packed around the cylinder, then it would be hand churned until the contents turned to ice cream. The following kulfi recipe does involve a cooking step, which requires a little patience while you reduce the milk on the stove, and it is best frozen overnight, but it's well worth it. The result is a thick, creamy ice cream with a wonderful texture.

Spiced jaggery kulfi

SERVES 6

4¼ cups (1 liter) whole milk

1½ cups (375 ml) can evaporated milk

10–15 cardamom pods, seeds removed and crushed

pinch of saffron plus extra to decorate

3½ oz (100 g) jaggery or ½ cup (100 g) brown sugar*

¼ cup (50 g) sugar

In a large heavy-based pot, heat the milk, evaporated milk, crushed cardamom seeds and saffron over medium heat and bring to a boil. Lower the heat and allow to simmer gently for at least 1 hour or until it has reduced by half. You will need to stir every 10–15 minutes. Once the mixture has reduced, add the jaggery and sugar and simmer for another 10 minutes.

Leave to cool, then transfer into bowls to freeze for at least 12 hours or overnight. Decorate each one with saffron strands.

* Jaggery, available at most Indian grocery stores, is unrefined sugar made from sugar cane juice. It has a wonderful rich flavor, but if necessary you can substitute brown sugar.

This is a great pie to add to your repertoire. It's fragrant and delicious, with crumpled layers of crunchy, buttery filo, and so simple to make. I find it amazing that just a touch of saffron can turn the color of the fruit to an intense orange. I use a 10 in (25 cm) cast-iron ovenproof skillet to cook the fruit and bake the pie, but if you don't have one of these, simply transfer the softened fruit to a pie dish before topping with the filo.

Apricot, peach, honey & saffron pie

SERVES 6–8

8–10 peaches and apricots, halved and pitted

7–14 tablespoons (100–200 g) butter

1–2 tablespoons honey

pinch of saffron

5–6 sheets filo pastry*

confectioners' sugar to dust

whipped cream or Greek-style yogurt to serve

Preheat the oven to 350°F (180°C).

Roughly chop the fruit. Melt 1 tablespoon of the butter in an ovenproof cast-iron skillet or ovenproof pan and add the fruit. Allow it to soften slightly, then add the honey and saffron and cook on medium heat for about 10 minutes until soft.

Melt the remaining butter. Using a pastry brush, brush each sheet of filo with melted butter and crumple it on top of the fruit, ensuring the edges are tucked under the fruit. Repeat until you have brushed and crumpled all of the pastry.

Bake for 30–35 minutes or until golden. Remove from the oven and set aside to cool.

Before serving, dust liberally with confectioners' sugar and serve with a dollop of whipped cream or Greek-style yogurt.

* Keep the filo pastry wrapped in a damp tea towel as you work to prevent it from drying out.

This is an amazing pie to make when cherries are in season, but if you are making it out of season you can use frozen pitted cherries. Use any pie dish, but I like to use a fluted loose-bottomed rectangular 5 x 13 in (12 x 34 cm) tart pan.

Cherry pie

SERVES 6–8

- **2 sheets (1 lb/500 g) sweet shortcrust pastry**
- **3/4 cup (150 g) sugar (preferably superfine)**
- **2 tablespoons cornstarch**
- **1 teaspoon ground cinnamon**
- **1 teaspoon vanilla extract**
- **1/2 teaspoon almond extract**
- **2 lb 3 oz (1 kg) cherries, pitted, stems removed**
- **1 tablespoon milk**
- **2 tablespoons sugar**
- **whipped cream or ice cream to serve**

Preheat the oven to 350°F (180°C).

Grease a pie dish or tart pan well and line it with a sheet of pastry. Trim the edges, joining it as necessary, but if it tears, just squish the edges together—this kind of pastry is quite forgiving. Reserve any leftover pastry to make decorative strips.

In a large bowl, combine the sugar, cornstarch, cinnamon, vanilla, and almond extract. Stir in the cherries.

Pour the cherry mixture into the pie dish and decorate with the reserved pastry strips (I have done a lattice pattern). Brush the pastry with the milk and sprinkle with the sugar.

Bake for 30–35 minutes or until the pastry is golden. Remove from the oven and set aside to cool just a little. Slice and serve hot with custard, cream or ice cream.

This is a perfect summer dessert after a barbecue. Make a day ahead so you have time to "rough" it up as it freezes.

Mandarin & cardamom granita

SERVES 6–8

3 x 11 oz (312 g) cans mandarin segments, drained

zest of 2 limes

2 tablespoons lime juice

handful of basil leaves, finely chopped, plus whole leaves to garnish

⅔ cup (130 g) white sugar

3–4 cardamom pods, crushed so they are slightly open

basil leaves to garnish

In a blender or food processor, blend the mandarin segments to a purée. Strain into a bowl orpitcher, then stir in the lime zest, lime juice and basil.

In a small saucepan, gently heat the sugar, cardamom and 1 cup (250 ml) of water until the sugar completely dissolves. Increase the heat and boil for a minute or so. Remove from the heat and allow to cool for a few minutes.

Mix the cooled syrup with the mandarin juice (discard the cardamom pods if you like, or keep them in; they make the mixture smell divine).

Pour into a shallow container and place in the freezer. Use a fork to rough up the granita every hour or two. To serve, scrape the granita into small glasses, top with basil leaves and serve immediately.

This yogurt drink, traditionally served with spicy food in India, quenches your thirst and helps with digestion. Lassi originated in the Punjab, where it is stored in earthenware pots to keep cool. It can be flavored with fruit or salt and spices.

Lime, lychee & rose water lassi

MAKES ABOUT 4¼ CUPS (1 LITER)

- ¼ cup (50 g) sugar
- 1 cup (180 g) canned lychees, plus ½ cup (120 ml) of the juice
- juice of 2 limes
- 2 cups (450 g) plain yogurt
- 1 teaspoon rose water
- ¼ teaspoon ground cardamom
- edible dried rose petals to decorate

Place all the ingredients, except the rose petals, into a blender with 1 cup (240 ml) of water and process until smooth and frothy. Serve the lassi chilled, over ice, decorated with rose petals.

This pretty tart, made with a store-bought pastry crust, is so simple to whip up.

Strawberry, elderflower & cardamom tart

SERVES 4–6

½ cup (120 ml) elderflower syrup

2–3 green cardamom pods, partly crushed

1 lb (500 g) fresh strawberries, hulled and sliced or halved

1–1⅓ cups (250–300 g) mascarpone

1–2 tablespoons confectioners' sugar

½ teaspoon vanilla extract

fresh mint leaves and confectioners' sugar to garnish (optional)

8–9½ in (20–24 cm) ready-made no-bake pie crust

In a small saucepan, bring the syrup, cardamom pods and ¼ cup (60 ml) of water to a boil. Reduce heat and leave to simmer for 5 minutes before setting aside to cool completely. Once cooled, remove the cardamom pods.

Place the strawberries in a bowl. Pour the elderflower syrup over the berries and refrigerate until needed.

Lightly whisk the mascarpone with the confectioners' sugar and vanilla until combined. Spoon this mixture into the pie crust in thick pillowy dollops. Scatter the marinated strawberries over the mascarpone and drizzle with the syrup. Garnish with the mint leaves and confectioners' sugar if desired.

This book is all about creating easy, simple recipes to encourage you to try flavors and spices you might not usually use, such as in this easy, no-churn ice cream. Ideal for summer entertaining, it takes no time to prepare—and you can replace the nuts and berries with chopped chocolate or other flavors as you wish.

Pistachio, raspberry & rose semifreddo

SERVES 6

2½ cups (600 ml) heavy cream

1¼ cups (300 ml) sweetened condensed milk

½ cup (70 g) chopped pistachios

1 teaspoon rose water

½–¾ cup (60–90 g) fresh raspberries

raspberries, chopped nuts, edible dried rose petals, and cotton candy to garnish

In a bowl or mixer, whisk the cream until it starts to thicken, then slowly add the condensed milk. Stir in the chopped pistachios and rose water and whisk a little more, taking care not to over-mix.

Fold in the berries, then pour into your desired container and decorate with the reserved berries, nuts and rose petals.

Freeze overnight for best results, but you can get away with 4–6 hours if you need to serve it sooner.

Garnish with cotton candy just before serving if desired.

"Season of mists and mellow fruitfulness, close bosom-friend of the maturing sun . . ."

JOHN KEATS

Fall

These first two lines of one of my favorite poems by John Keats best sums up this chapter for me. It's about cool evenings by the fire; hearty dinners followed by warm apple hand pies or a homemade tart oozing a luscious saffron-colored sweet jam. Hot cinnamon pears encrusted in flaky pastry fill the air with the aroma of chai spices. Make the most of this season full of tasty apples and pears. Adding a hint of spice is guaranteed to bring warmth and flavor to your fall.

With only a handful of ingredients these impressive-looking pies can be made with ease, making for a fun and very beautiful recipe. They will make a great talking point at any party.

Rose apple pies

MAKES 10

juice of 1 lemon

4–6 apples, thinly sliced (a mandoline is best for this)

2 sheets frozen puff pastry, thawed

3 tablespoons strawberry or apricot jam

¼ cup (50 g) raw sugar

½ teaspoon ground cinnamon

honey and mascarpone to serve

Preheat the oven to 375°F (190°C). Grease and chill a 12-hole muffin pan.

Half-fill a large microwave-safe bowl with water and add the lemon juice. Add the sliced apples so they don't lose their color. Microwave the apple slices for 2–3 minutes to make them pliable and easy to roll.

Cut each sheet of pastry into 5 strips, each roughly 1½ in (4 cm) wide.

In a small bowl, combine the jam and 2 tablespoons of water. Microwave for 1 minute. Spread a thin layer of the diluted jam on each pastry strip. Arrange the apple slices along the top of the strip, horizontally, making sure they overlap each other. Fold the bottom half of the pastry up to encase the slices.

Working with one strip at a time and starting from one end, roll up the enclosed apples to form a rose. Place each rose in the prepared muffin pan.

Mix together the raw sugar and cinnamon and sprinkle over the tops of the pies.

Bake for 35–40 minutes or until the pastry is cooked (if the apples are browning too much, cover the top with foil to prevent them from burning).

Serve hot with a drizzle of honey and a dollop of mascarpone.

I have memories of eating this jam tart when I was growing up in Malawi. Back then pastries weren't easily sourced and my mom made everything herself, including this tart, which she'd make with strawberry jam. Here I've given it a Kiwi twist—incorporating the feijoa and saffron jam that I have loved making ever since I discovered a feijoa tree fruiting in my backyard. The saffron not only gives an intense orange color but also adds a lovely flowery note. You can use any jam you like, but be sure to make it ahead of time.

Mom's jam tart bars with feijoa & saffron jam

SERVES 8

2 sticks (225 g) butter, softened
⅔ cup (120 g) sugar
2 eggs
3¾ cups (450 g) all-purpose flour, plus extra for dusting
¼ cup (30 g) self-rising flour
1 teaspoon vanilla extract
milk for brushing
whipped cream to serve

FEIJOA AND SAFFRON JAM
(MAKES 2 X PINT-SIZE/500 ML JARS)

2 lb 3 oz (1 kg) feijoas*
2–3 cardamom pods, crushed until open
generous pinch of saffron
zest of 1 lemon
juice of ½ lemon
1 cup (200 g) sugar

To make the jam, scoop out the flesh of the feijoas and roughly chop. Place in a large pot with the spices, ¼ cup (60 ml) of water, and lemon zest and juice and boil gently for about 10 minutes or until the fruit is soft. Add the sugar and boil for 10–15 minutes or until thick and syrupy. Transfer to clean jars and allow to cool before covering (store leftovers in the refrigerator).

Preheat the oven to 375°F (190°C). Grease a baking sheet. Beat together the butter and sugar until light and fluffy. Add the eggs and sift in both flours, then mix in the vanilla until you have a soft dough. Transfer to a floured surface and knead to bring it together. Cut off three-quarters of the dough and roll out to a 8 x 12 in (20 x 30 cm) rectangle. Place on the greased pan.

Spread 1–1½ cups (340–500 g) of the jam over the pastry sheet. Roll out the remaining dough and cut into strips about ½ in (1.5 cm) wide. Lay the strips over the jam to make a lattice pattern, then brush with a little milk.

Bake for 35–40 minutes or until golden. Cut into squares and serve with a dollop of freshly whipped cream.

*Feijoas are also known as pineapple guava, fig guava or guavasteen and are grown in South America, California, and New Zealand. You can find them in late fall, or substitute ripe pears.

In our family we have always eaten dates, particularly during the month of Ramadan when they are used to break the fast at the end of each day. This recipe makes a perfect lunch or after-school treat all-year round. And the chocolate coating makes a great topping for ice cream, too.

Medjool dates with peanut butter chocolate

SERVES 4–6

10–12 whole Medjool dates
½–1 cup (120–230 g) thick whipped cream or mascarpone
freeze-dried crushed raspberries

CHOCOLATE COATING

¼ cup (70 g) crunchy peanut butter
½ cup (90 g) milk or dark chocolate chips

Cut each date lengthwise and remove the pit. Fill the cavities with cream, then set aside.

To make the chocolate coating, melt the peanut butter and chocolate chips in the microwave and mix the peanut butter in.

Using a pair of tweezers or tongs, dip each date in the chocolate mixture and place on a wire rack until set. Sprinkle with the dried raspberries and refrigerate until ready to eat.

Turmeric has natural anti-inflammatory and anti-oxidant properties in the form of curcumin, and has been used for centuries in India for its medicinal properties. When I was a child in Malawi, at the first sign of a cold, Mom would give us this hot milky drink. These days I love drinking it at the beginning of the colder months as it helps to keep the immune system in good condition for winter.

Turmeric & ginger latte

SERVES 2–3

2 cups (500 ml) milk (can be plant/nut-based)

¾ teaspoon turmeric (ground or freshly grated)

¼ teaspoon ground cinnamon, plus extra to serve

small piece of fresh ginger root, grated

pinch of black pepper

1 teaspoon honey or maple syrup (optional)

pinch of saffron (optional)

In a saucepan, gently heat the milk. Add the turmeric, cinnamon, ginger and black pepper and heat until the mixture just starts to boil. Simmer for 6–8 minutes.

Stir in the honey or maple syrup, if using. Remove from the heat and strain into glasses or cups.

Sprinkle with the saffron, if using, and additional cinnamon if you wish.

Chaa or chai is a milky tea made with spices, served in every Indian home. Each family has its own version, with different spices. In Western countries it's called chai tea or chai latte, however, because chai means tea, asking for chai tea is like asking for "tea tea." Masala (spice) chai is, in my opinion, the most appropriate name for it. For a dairy-free option, make it with nut or soy milk.

Masala chaa

SERVES 2

- 1 x 2 in (5 cm) cinnamon stick
- 1 star anise
- 3–4 cloves
- 4–6 cardamom pods
- 3–4 peppercorns
- 1 cup (250 ml) milk (can be plant/nut-based)
- 3–4 English breakfast tea bags or loose-leaf tea if preferred
- 1 small piece of fresh ginger, finely sliced
- 1 tablespoon sugar (or honey or maple syrup)

Lightly crush the spices and place them in a saucepan with 1 cup (250 ml) of water. Add the milk, tea bags, ginger and sugar. Bring to a boil, then turn down the heat and simmer for 5 minutes. Strain into cups and serve hot.

This delightful recipe comes from my sister, Effie. She's married to a French chef so needless to say, cooking is his domain, but this is one of her recipes. Similar to shortbread, these delicate melt-in-your-mouth cookies pair well with a cup of tea on a blustery fall day.

Effie's softies

MAKES ABOUT 30

18 tablespoons (250 g) butter, softened

⅓ cup (80 ml) neutral oil

¾ cup (85 g) confectioners' sugar, plus extra to dust

1 cup (115 g) cornstarch

2½ cups (300 g) all-purpose flour, sifted

Preheat the oven to 350°F (180°C). Line a baking sheet with parchment paper.

Whisk the butter, oil and confectioners' sugar together until pale. Add the cornstarch and the sifted flour. Mix well to form a soft dough.

Divide the dough into quarters and roll out to form four long rectangles, each about 12 x 1 in (30 x 3 cm). Place on a tray, cover with a damp cloth and refrigerate for 30 minutes.

Remove from the fridge and slice each piece into smaller 1 x 2 in (3 x 5 cm) rectangles. Place on the prepared pan and bake for 20–25 minutes until pale (they shouldn't have too much color).

Allow to cool, then dust with confectioners' sugar.

Muffins are one of my favorite things to eat with a cup tea in the morning. Hot out of the oven, slathered with butter, what's not to like? This easy recipe also works well with berries.

Feijoa muffins

MAKES 12 SMALL OR 6 LARGE

2 cups (240 g) all-purpose flour
4 teaspoons baking powder
½ cup (100 g) sugar
¼ teaspoon salt
7 tablespoons (100 g) butter, melted, plus extra to serve
1 cup (120 ml) milk
1 egg
1 cup (175 g) chopped feijoas (see page 59) or berries
1 tablespoon raw sugar
½ teaspoon ground cinnamon

Preheat the oven to 425°F (220°C).

Grease a 12-hole muffin pan (or a large 6-hole one).

Sift the dry ingredients into a bowl. In another bowl, combine the melted butter, milk and egg and lightly whisk. Add the chopped feijoas to the wet ingredients mixture. Gently fold the wet ingredients into the dry ingredients, taking care not to over-mix. Spoon the mixture into the prepared muffin pan.

Mix the raw sugar with the cinnamon and sprinkle over each muffin.

Bake for 12–15 minutes until the muffins spring back when lightly touched.

Serve hot with butter.

Rhubarb is just coming into season in late summer/early fall in New Zealand, but I often freeze it for year-round use. Given it's still warm enough occasionally to indulge in ice cream at this time of year, I highly recommend this gorgeous flavor combination that packs a punch, with spicy undertones of star anise and the tart sweetness of rhubarb. As it's a no-churn ice cream, it's easy to whip up and take out of the freezer when you need it.

Rhubarb & star-anise ice cream

SERVES 6–8

1 lb (450 g) rhubarb (fresh or frozen)
¾ cup (150 g) sugar
1 whole star anise
2 cups (500 ml) whipping cream
a squeeze of lemon juice

In a pot, cook the rhubarb, sugar and star anise over medium heat for 10–12 minutes or until the sugar has dissolved.

Discard the star anise, then blend while still in the pot (an immersion blender is perfect for this). Refrigerate for 15 minutes.

Whip the cream until soft peaks form. Add the lemon juice to the rhubarb and then fold the rhubarb into the cream.

Scoop into a container and freeze for at least 6 hours before serving.

This is the easiest loaf to make if you are in a rush, using bananas that are just starting to turn brown. Keep over-ripe bananas in the freezer so you have them on hand for this recipe.

Caramelized banana & cinnamon loaf

SERVES 6–8

1¾ cups (215 g) self-rising flour

¼ teaspoon baking soda

pinch of salt

½ cup (100 g) sugar

2 eggs

5 tbsp (75 g) butter, melted

¼ cup (60 ml) hot milk

2–3 ripe bananas, mashed (about 1 cup)

TOPPING

1 banana, peeled and halved lengthwise

½ teaspoon ground cinnamon

1 tablespoon raw sugar

butter to serve

Preheat the oven to 350°F (180°C).

Grease and line a 9½ x 5 in (24 x 12 cm) loaf pan or equivalent cake pan.

Sift the flour, baking soda and salt into a large bowl and add the sugar.

In a separate bowl, beat the eggs. Add the melted butter, hot milk and mashed banana to the eggs and stir into the dry mixture until just combined. Take care not to overmix at this stage. Pour the mixture into the prepared pan.

Place the two banana halves cut side down lengthwise on top. Mix the cinnamon and raw sugar and sprinkle over to make a crunchy topping.

Bake for 45–50 minutes or until a skewer comes out clean. Leave to cool and then turn out onto a wire rack.

Serve warm, spread with butter.

Gulab jamun, dough balls made from milk solids which are fried and then soaked in a sweet rose-flavored syrup, are an extremely popular Indian sweet. Similar to mini doughnuts, the name means "rose-flavored plum." They make a very pretty dessert, which I like to serve with whipped cream or mascarpone. But be warned: you will not stop at one—they are dangerously divine.

Gulab jamun with cardamom & rose syrup

MAKES 12–14

SYRUP

2 cups (400 g) sugar

4–6 drops rose water

1–2 cardamom pods, crushed

GULAB JAMUN

scant 1 cup (100 g) powdered milk

2 tablespoons self-rising flour

2 teaspoons fine semolina

2 tablespoons ghee

¼ cup (60 ml) milk

oil for frying

TO SERVE

thick whipped cream or mascarpone

edible dried rose petals, edible gold dust (optional)

To make the syrup, combine the sugar and 4 cups (950 ml) of water in a large heavy-based pot over medium heat and stir until the sugar dissolves. Bring to a boil and add the rose water and cardamom pods. Remove from the heat and set aside to cool.

To make the gulab jamun, mix together the powdered milk, flour, semolina and ghee in a bowl. Add enough milk to make a soft dough and mix until smooth. Using your hands, roll out the dough and divide into 12–14 portions. Form each portion into a small ball.

Add enough oil to a deep pot or karahi (Indian wok), so that it is about one-third full and heat to 350-375°F (180-190°C) (it will be hot enough to cook the dough balls when a a small piece of bread dropped into the oil turns golden after a minute).

Fry the balls, a few at a time, until they turn a dark golden color all over. Using a slotted spoon, remove them from the hot oil and carefully drop into the syrup. Bring the syrup back to a boil, then remove from the heat.

Transfer the gulab jamun to a large serving bowl or small bowls, drizzle with some of the syrup, and set aside to cool.

Garnish with dried rose petals and edible gold dust if desired and serve at room temperature with a dollop of whipped cream or mascarpone.

These lovely, zesty little cakes with lime and a touch of saffron are even better when enjoyed with a cup of tea.

Coconut, lime & saffron cakes

MAKES 12

5 egg whites
1½ cups (170 g) confectioners' sugar
½ cup (60 g) all-purpose flour
scant 1 cup (70 g) ground almonds
pinch of saffron
1 cup (85 g) desiccated coconut
1 tablespoon grated lime zest
11 tablespoons (150 g) butter, melted

LIME FROSTING

1 cup (250 g) mascarpone
confectioners' sugar to taste
squeeze of lime juice and zest of 1 lime
saffron strands and honey to decorate (optional)

Preheat the oven to 350°F (180°C). Grease a 12-hole muffin pan.

In a large bowl or mixer, beat the egg whites until soft peaks form.

In a separate bowl, sift together the confectioners' sugar and flour. Add the ground almonds, saffron, coconut and lime zest. Fold the dry mixture and the melted butter into the egg whites, folding until combined.

Spoon the mixture into the prepared muffin pan. Bake for 15–20 minutes or until they spring back when lightly touched. Allow to cool slightly before transferring to wire racks.

To make the frosting, whip the mascarpone with the confectioners' sugar and lime juice and zest until light. Dollop the frosting onto the cooled cakes and decorate with a couple of saffron strands, then drizzle with honey, if desired.

A stunning sweet treat with a rich and decadent flavor and simply amazing color. It's another version of my Carrot Halva (see page 75) and while it takes time and patience it's definitely worth it. I've included this version as I feel it is a really great blend of my cultures.

Beet halva

SERVES 4–6

5 cups (1.2 liters) milk
7 oz (200 g) beets, peeled and grated
3–4 cardamom pods
5 tbsp (75 g) butter
¾ cup (150 g) sugar
whipped cream or yogurt to serve

Place the milk and grated beets in a heavy-based pot and cook over medium–low heat, stirring occasionally, for up to 1 hour or until the liquid has evaporated. Watch it carefully for the last 15 minutes or so to ensure it's not sticking to the bottom of the pot.

Crush the cardamom pods and extract the black seeds. Grind the seeds in a mortar and pestle.

Add the butter, sugar and crushed cardamom seeds to the pot. Stir with a wooden spoon until the butter has melted and the sugar has dissolved.

Cook for a further 15–20 minutes, stirring frequently, until the mixture starts to leave the side of the pot. Watch closely to ensure the sugar doesn't burn.

Serve in small dishes with a dollop of whipped cream or yogurt.

Halva is a dense Indian sweet dessert made with sweet vegetables, fruits or flours and flavored with anything from spices to extracts and nuts. There are also Middle Eastern and Greek versions. My recipe is for a classic Indian halva made with carrots, often served for special occasions like weddings. Sticky and sweet with a gorgeous caramelized flavor, it's delicious served with mascarpone, which cuts through the sweetness. Raisins are a traditional ingredient, but here I've made them optional.

Carrot halva with mascarpone

SERVES 4

5 cups (1.2 liters) milk

9 oz (250 g) carrots, peeled and grated

¼ teaspoon ground cardamom

5 tbsp (75 g) butter

scant 1 cup (170 g) sugar

¼–½ cup (40–80 g) raisins (optional)

mascarpone to serve

½ cup (50 g) crushed pistachios to serve

In a heavy-based pot, cook the milk, carrot and cardamom over medium–low heat, stirring occasionally, for 25–30 minutes until all the liquid has evaporated. Watch it carefully; you don't want it to catch on the bottom of the pot.

Add the butter and sugar to the pot, along with the raisins, if using, and stir with a wooden spoon until the butter has melted and the sugar has dissolved.

Cook for a further 10–15 minutes, stirring frequently, until the mixture starts to leave the side of the pot. Watch it closely until the mixture becomes dry and sticky and you see a change in color, which tells you that it's ready.

Transfer the mixture to a dish or divide into four small (¼-cup/60 ml capacity) ramekins or molds.

Set aside to cool, then turn out and serve with a dollop of mascarpone and a sprinkle of pistachios.

Baklava is a traditional Middle Eastern and Mediterranean treat, with many variations. I love the simple use of nuts, crunchy filo and the sweetness of the fragrant syrup holding it all together. It looks so pretty, too, sprinkled with dried rose petals. You can just use one variety of nut or a combination.

Rose, saffron & orange-blossom baklava

MAKES 18–20 PIECES

2 cups (250 g) pistachios
2 cups (200 g) mixed nuts (e.g., almonds, walnuts, hazelnuts)
¼ cup (50 g) sugar
1 teaspoon ground cinnamon
½ teaspoon ground cardamom
9 tablespoons (125 g) butter, melted, plus extra for greasing
12 sheets filo pastry*

SYRUP

½ cup (120 ml) honey
½ cup (100 g) sugar
2 teaspoons rose water
2 teaspoons orange blossom water
pinch of saffron
edible dried rose petals to garnish

Preheat the oven to 350°F (180°C). Grease a 9 in (23 cm) square cake pan with melted butter.

Place the nuts in a food processor and pulse until finely chopped. Transfer to a large bowl, add the sugar and the spices and stir to combine.

Place a sheet of filo pastry on a clean work surface and brush with melted butter. Cover with two more layers of filo, brushed with butter, then place into the pan and fold the edges to fit. Sprinkle a layer of spiced nuts over top. Prepare three more layers of buttered filo and place them on top of the nut layer. Repeat the process with the remaining filo pastry and nut mixture, ending with a layer of filo.

Using a sharp knife, score the filo into diamond shapes all the way through to the bottom of the pan. Bake for 35–40 minutes or until golden.

Meanwhile, make the syrup. In a pot, combine the honey, ½ cup (120 ml) of water and the sugar over medium–high heat until the sugar dissolves. Cook until the syrup thickens, then remove from the heat. Add the rose water, orange blossom water and saffron. Stir to combine and set aside.

Remove from the oven and pour the syrup all over the baklava. Allow to cool completely, then garnish with dried rose petals and serve with a cup of apple tea.

* Keep the filo pastry wrapped in a damp tea towel as you work to prevent it from drying out.

I love any dessert with cream. Add a crackle on top and I am in heaven. This Indian spiced brûlée offers the flavors of a traditional Indian ice cream called kulfi, often flavored with pistachios and cardamom.

Cardamom kulfi brûlée

SERVES 6

- **2½ cups (600 ml) heavy cream**
- **6–8 whole cardamom pods, slightly crushed**
- **1 cinnamon stick**
- **6 egg yolks**
- **⅓ cup (70 g) sugar (preferably superfine), plus extra for topping**

Preheat the oven to 325°F (160°C).

In a pot, heat the cream and spices over medium heat for 5–6 minutes until almost boiling. Remove from the heat and set aside to allow the spices to infuse.

In a bowl or mixer, whisk the egg yolks and sugar until pale and foamy. Strain the cream mixture and add to the egg yolk mixture. Stir until combined.

Divide the mixture between 6 x ⅔-cup (150 ml) ramekins. Place the ramekins in a roasting pan and pour boiling water into the pan to come halfway up the sides of the ramekins.

Bake for 30–35 minutes until just set. Remove the ramekins from the oven and set aside to cool before refrigerating for 3–4 hours or overnight.

Before serving, sprinkle the top of each with extra sugar and use a brûlée blow torch or place under a hot broiler until the sugar caramelizes. Take care that the sugar does not burn. Put them back in the fridge until you are ready to serve.

This is a rich chocolate mousse flavored with cardamom. These stunning little desserts are best served in small shot glasses. They make a perfect after-dinner treat.

Chocolate & cardamom puddings

SERVES 8

1¼ cups (300 ml) heavy cream
7 oz (200 g) dark chocolate, chopped
2–3 cardamom pods, seeds removed and crushed
pinch of ground cinnamon
2 egg yolks
scant 1 cup (200 g) mascarpone
whipped cream and chopped pistachios to serve

In a pot, gently heat the cream over medium heat until it starts to simmer. Remove from the heat, add the chopped chocolate and whisk until melted.

Add the cardamom to the chocolate mixture, along with the cinnamon. Whisk the egg yolks into the mixture and then whisk in the mascarpone.

Divide the mixture among small glasses and refrigerate for 4–6 hours or until set. Decorate with whipped cream and chopped pistachios.

This recipe comes from my sister Nishat, whom we fondly call Nini. It's a Middle Eastern and Mediterranean dessert that has many variations, depending on where you come from. Nini's version uses mozzarella and a beautiful rose-flavored syrup.

Nini's kanafa

SERVES 4–6

11 tablespoons (150 g) butter, melted, plus extra for greasing

9–10½ oz (250–300 g) kataifi pastry*

1 cup (250 g) mascarpone

1 teaspoon rose water

1 teaspoon orange blossom water

1–2 tablespoons confectioners' sugar or to taste

½ cup (50 g) chopped pistachios, or other nuts

3½–5 oz (100–150 g) fresh mozzarella

SYRUP

1 cup (200 g) sugar

1 teaspoon lemon juice

1 teaspoon rose water

1 teaspoon orange blossom water

nuts and edible dried rose petals to decorate

ice cream or cream to serve

Preheat the oven to 350°F (180°C). Grease a cake pan or pans with butter (use four mini springform cake pans for individual servings or a 9–9½ in/22–24 cm cake pan for one large kanafa).

Cut the shredded kataifi pastry into short lengths and place in a bowl. Add the melted butter and toss lightly to coat the strands. Place half of the pastry in the prepared pan/s in an even layer. Flatten the pastry with the bottom of a cup.

In another bowl, mix the mascarpone with the flower waters and confectioners' sugar. Spread the mascarpone mixture over the flattened pastry, then sprinkle with the chopped nuts. Shred the mozzarella and sprinkle over the top. Cover with the remaining buttered pastry, pressing it down and making sure none of the filling is visible.

Place the cake pan/s on a baking sheet to prevent any melted butter dripping onto the bottom of your oven. Bake for 30 minutes or until golden.

Combine the ingredients for the syrup with ½ cup (120 ml) of water in a small saucepan and boil until you have a thick syrup. Just before serving, pour the syrup over the kanafa and decorate with nuts and dried rose petals. Serve hot with ice cream or cream.

* Kataifi (shredded filo pastry) comes in fine strands and is available from Greek, Turkish, and Middle Eastern grocery stores and some supermarkets.

The taste of these fritters takes me back to my childhood when my mom used to make them. They're just the thing to make when you've got over-ripe bananas.

Cinnamon banana fritti

SERVES 6

½ cup (120 ml) milk
2 bananas, mashed
2 cups (250 g) all-purpose flour
2 teaspoons sugar, plus ½ cup (100 g) extra for dusting
½ teaspoon salt
1 tablespoon baking powder
2 eggs, beaten
1 tablespoon butter, melted
vegetable oil for frying
½ teaspoon ground cinnamon
¼ teaspoon ground cardamom
ice cream to serve

In a large mixing bowl, combine the milk and bananas. Sift in the flour, 2 teaspoons of sugar, salt and baking powder. Add the eggs and butter and mix well.

Place enough oil in a pan or small wok so that it is about one-third full and heat to about 270°F (130°C) (Add a drop of batter; if it sizzles the oil is ready.)

Carefully drop small teaspoonsful of the mixture into the hot oil, keeping it at a steady heat. Fry until golden, making sure each one is cooked on all sides. Remove with a slotted spoon and drain on paper towels.

Mix the ½ cup (100 g) of sugar with the cinnamon and cardamom. Dust the fritters with the spiced sugar and serve hot with ice cream.

This is my take on the apple hand pie. The added spice just elevates the taste.

Chai-spiced apple turnovers

MAKES 12–14

¼ cup (50 g) sugar (preferably superfine)
½ teaspoon ground cinnamon
¼ teaspoon ground nutmeg
¼ teaspoon ground cardamom
12 oz (350 g) peeled and thinly sliced tart apples (Granny Smiths work well)
2–3 whole cloves
small piece of cinnamon stick
generous squeeze of lemon juice
3–4 sheets frozen puff pastry, thawed
3 tbsp (50 g) butter, cut into small pieces
milk or water for sealing the pastry
confectioners' sugar for dusting

Preheat the oven to 375°F (190°C). To make the filling, combine the sugar, ground cinnamon, nutmeg and cardamom in a small bowl and set aside.

In a large pot, combine the sliced apples, cloves and cinnamon stick, ½ cup (120 ml) of water and the lemon juice. Cook, covered, for 8–10 minutes over low heat until the apples are tender, not mushy. Remove from the heat and drain.

Sprinkle the spiced sugar over the apples so they are well coated. Using a 4 in (10 cm) round pastry cutter, cut 4–6 circles out of each sheet of pastry. You should have 10–12 circles in total.

Place a spoonful of spiced apple mixture on each circle, then dot with a small piece of the butter. Moisten the edges of the pastry with a little milk or water, then fold to form a semi-circle. Using a fork or your fingers, firmly crimp the edges together.

Bake for 25–30 or until golden and puffy, then remove from the oven and dust with confectioners' sugar. Serve warm with your favorite ice cream.

Serve these pears when the weather is just turning and you want a fuss-free yet elegant dessert. Serve with ice cream and a drizzle of syrup.

Saffron-spiced pears in puff pastry

SERVES 4

- **4 small pears, just ripe and still firm**
- **2 cups (400 g) sugar**
- **¼ cup (80 g) honey**
- **½ lemon**
- **6–8 cardamom pods**
- **2 cinnamon sticks**
- **4–6 cloves**
- **pinch of saffron**
- **1 vanilla bean, split and seeds scraped**
- **2 sheets frozen puff pastry, thawed but chilled**
- **2 tablespoons sugar**
- **½ teaspoon ground cinnamon**
- **1 egg, lightly beaten**
- **ice cream to serve**

Preheat the oven to 400°F (200°C). Line a baking sheet with parchment paper.

Core and peel pears from the bottom to leave the stems intact. Level the base of each so they can stand up.

In a large pot, combine 4 cups (950 ml) of water, the sugar, honey, lemon, spices and vanilla bean and seeds and bring to a boil. Reduce the heat to a simmer and place the pears in the pot on their sides. Poach until tender, basting occasionally, for 18–20 minutes. Allow to cool slightly then place the pot in the fridge while you prepare the pastry.

Cut four small squares from one of the pastry sheets for the base of the pears to sit on. Cut the remaining pastry into 1–½ in (1.5 cm)-wide strips.

Using a slotted spoon, remove the pears from the liquid and set 1½ cups (350 ml) of the poaching liquid aside. Place each pear on a pastry square. Starting at the bottom of the pear, wrap a pastry strip around it until you get to the stem (you may need more than one strip). Repeat with the remaining pears and pastry.

Mix together the sugar and cinnamon. Brush the pastry strips with the beaten egg and sprinkle with the cinnamon sugar. Place the pears on the prepared pan, allowing plenty of room around each. Bake for 25–30 minutes or until golden brown.

Meanwhile, bring the reserved poaching liquid to a boil and cook until the liquid is thick and syrupy, about 10 minutes. Remove the pears from the oven and serve hot with ice cream and a drizzle of the poaching liquid.

Winter

I still find it hard to get used to winter in Auckland; the trees are not bare, there is no snow, but it's still a good time to hibernate in front of a cozy fire with a cup of chile hot chocolate and a satisfying dessert. In this chapter I will share with you desserts and baked treats that will bring you joy, comfort and nostalgia, along with a touch of the East in the form of warming spices like star anise, ginger and cinnamon.

". . . And don't think the garden loses its ecstasy in winter. It's quiet but the roots are down there riotous."

RUMI

Early-season rhubarb is always delicious in pies and tarts . . . but it is next-level when used in this really simple brûlée. I freeze rhubarb to make this warming dessert whenever I fancy it.

Roasted rhubarb & ginger crème brûlée

SERVES 4

1 lb 12 oz (800 g) rhubarb (fresh or frozen)

3 tablespoons brown sugar, plus 1–2 tablespoons extra for the brûlée

2 teaspoons ground ginger

2 pieces stem ginger, finely chopped (or use crystallized/candied ginger)

½ teaspoon ground cinnamon

1¼ cups (300 ml) heavy cream

scant 1 cup (200 g) Greek-style yogurt

1–2 tablespoons brown sugar, plus extra

Preheat the oven to 350°F (180°C).

Chop and trim the rhubarb into ¾–1 in (2–3 cm) chunks. In a bowl, combine the rhubarb with 3 tablespoons of the sugar, ground ginger, stem ginger and cinnamon and toss to coat. Transfer to a 9½ in (24 cm) baking dish and bake for 20 minutes. Remove from the oven and stir before baking for a further 10–15 minutes until tender.

Set aside to cool completely. Drain the juice.

Whip the heavy cream until thick. Combine with the yogurt and and spoon it evenly over the cooled rhubarb. Sprinkle the 1–2 tablespoons of sugar over the top.

If you have a kitchen blow torch, use it to caramelize the top of the brûlée. Otherwise, turn on your broiler and place the brûlée in the top rack, about 3 in (8 cm) from the broiler, until the sugar has melted, caramelized and turned a rich golden color, 6–8 minutes. Watch carefully to ensure it doesn't burn.

Cool and then refrigerate, covered with plastic wrap, until you are ready to serve.

My very first blog was named after this fruit. And because I love tamarillos so much I had to feature them as a star ingredient in at least one of my cakes. If you can't find them, you can easily replace them with pears or other fruit for this recipe, but I love using tamarillos as they create such a stunningly colorful cake. Make it gluten-free, too, if you like—just swap the flour for a gluten-free alternative or replace with more ground almonds. To make it without refined sugars, use maple syrup, agave or a neutral honey.

Upside-down tamarillo cake

SERVES 6–8, CAN BE MADE GLUTEN-FREE

2 tablespoons butter, melted
¼ teaspoon ground cinnamon
¼ cup (50 g) raw sugar
4–5 tamarillos, peeled & halved*
7 tablespoons (100 g) softened butter
½ cup (100 g) brown sugar
zest of 2 lemons
3 eggs
½ cup (60 g) all-purpose or gluten-free flour
½ cup ground almonds
1½ teaspoons baking powder (gluten free if needed)
2 tablespoons lemon juice
crème fraîche or yogurt to serve

Preheat the oven to 325°F (160°C). Line a 7–8½ in (18–21 cm) springform cake pan with parchment paper.

Drizzle the melted butter into the pan. Mix together the cinnamon and raw sugar and scatter into the pan, over the melted butter. Arrange the tamarillos, cut-side down, in the pan.

In a bowl or mixer, whisk or mix the softened butter, brown sugar and lemon zest together until pale and fluffy (this can be done with a wooden spoon). Add the eggs, one at a time, making sure they are incorporated fully between each addition. Stir in the flour, ground almonds, baking powder and lemon juice until smooth, taking care not to over-mix.

Pour the cake batter over the tamarillos. Bake for 45–50 minutes or until the cake is light golden and springs back when touched.

Remove from the oven and set aside to cool for a few minutes. Run a knife around the edges before releasing the spring at the side of the pan. Place a plate on top and carefully flip the pan so that the cake is upside-down on the plate. Remove the bottom of the pan and peel off the parchment paper. Serve warm with crème fraîche or yogurt.

* Look for tamarillos (tree tomatoes/tomate de árbol) in Caribbean and Latin American grocery stores and some supermarkets in fall and winter. To peel the tamarillos, plunge the fruit into boiling water for 2–3 minutes, after which the skins can be peeled off easily.

A refreshingly unique dessert with a hint of the East. The way Mom always made it involved cooking the milk until it was completely absorbed, leaving the vermicelli plump and creamy. Vermicelli is widely available in Indian grocery stores.

Sevu

SERVES 4–6

7 tablespoons (100 g) butter

3½ oz (100 g) dried thin vermicelli

1½ cups (350 ml) milk

1–2 cardamom pods

¼ cup (50 g) sugar

handful of chopped pistachios (optional)

whipped cream to serve

Melt the butter in a large frying pan. Add the vermicelli and fry, stirring, until it turns a lovely golden color. Add the milk and cardamom pods and cook over low heat until the liquid has been absorbed. Add the sugar and cook until caramelized, 6–8 minutes.

Serve warm with chopped nuts if desired and a dollop of whipped cream.

The syrup makes these little cakes special. I make them in small 1-cup (200 ml) glass molds, but they work just as well when baked in a large muffin pan.

Baby pistachio cakes with star-anise orange syrup

MAKES 8

- 11 tbsp (150 g) butter, softened, plus extra for greasing
- 1¼ cups (360 ml) sweetened condensed milk
- 1¾ cups (150 g) ground pistachios
- 2 cups (260 g) all-purpose flour
- 1 teaspoon baking powder
- 1 teaspoon baking soda
- 2–3 drops orange blossom water

ORANGE SYRUP

- zest and juice of 2 oranges
- 6 tablespoons (75 g) sugar
- 1 star anise
- sugar for dusting
- handful of chopped pistachios
- crème fraîche to serve

Preheat the oven to 375°F (190°C). Line the bottom of eight ovenproof ramekins or 8 holes of a muffin pan and grease the sides well with butter.

In a bowl, beat together the condensed milk and butter until thick and creamy. Add 1 cup (240 ml) of water along with the ground pistachios, baking powder, baking soda, and orange blossom water and stir to combine. Spoon the thick mixture evenly into the molds and bake for 25 minutes or until a skewer inserted into the center of one comes out clean. Remove from the oven and turn out onto individual dessert plates.

To make the syrup, combine the zest and juice, sugar and star anise in a saucepan over medium heat and bring to boil. Simmer until thick and syrupy. Pour the hot syrup over the warm cakes. Dust with sugar, decorate with pistachios and serve with a dollop of crème fraîche.

Kheeraj (or rice pudding as we know it here in New Zealand) is a popular dish in the East as well as the West. This version, using rose water and saffron, takes rice pudding to another level. Enjoy it hot or cold.

Kheeraj with Medjool dates & pistachios

SERVES 6–8

1 cup (200 g) basmati rice

1 tablespoon ghee or butter

4 cups (950 ml) milk

1–2 drops rose water

pinch of saffron

¼ cup (40 g) raisins

1–1¼ cups (240–300 ml) sweetened condensed milk

chopped pistachios and Medjool dates to garnish

heavy cream to serve

Wash and soak the rice in water for 1 hour.

Drain the rice and add to a large pot along with the ghee, milk and 4 cups (950 ml) of water. Bring to a boil and then reduce the heat to low. Simmer gently until all the liquid has been absorbed (45 minutes–1 hour). Watch it at this stage to ensure it doesn't stick to the bottom of the pot.

Add the rose water, saffron, raisins and condensed milk to taste (use less if you don't want it too sweet). Stir to combine.

Serve warm, cold or at room temperature, garnished with pistachios and dates. Serve heavy cream on the side.

These deliciously light little cookies with their citrusy flavor go so well with a cup of tea and always remind me of winter. You can use oranges if you prefer.

Vanilla & mandarin cookies with poppy seed sugar

MAKES 14–16

8 oz (225 g) butter, softened
½ cup confectioners' sugar, sifted
½ teaspoon vanilla extract
or seeds from 1 vanilla bean
2 teaspoons mandarin juice
grated zest of 1 mandarin
2 cups flour, sifted

POPPY SEED SUGAR

90g confectioners' sugar
1 teaspoon poppy seeds

Preheat the oven to 325°F (170°C). Grease or line 1–2 baking sheets.

In a bowl or mixer, whisk the butter and confectioners' sugar until pale and fluffy. Add the vanilla and whisk for 1 minute. Add the mandarin juice and zest and mix through. Finally, fold in the flour.

Arrange heaped teaspoons of the mixture on the prepared baking sheets and shape into crescents. Bake for 20–25 minutes, taking care that they don't color too much.

Meanwhile, mix the confectioners' sugar and poppy seeds.

Remove the cookies from the oven and set aside to cool. Dust with the poppy seed sugar when cool.

Indulgent and comforting with a rich, creamy taste and a slight kick from the chile, it's best enjoyed at the fireside with toasted marshmallows. Although this recipe only makes enough for two people, it can easily be doubled.

Spicy hot chocolate

SERVES 2

- **3½ oz (100 g) dark chocolate, coarsely chopped**
- **1½ cups (350 ml) whole milk**
- **⅔ cup (150 ml) heavy cream**
- **½ teaspoon ground cinnamon**
- **¼ teaspoon ground chile powder**
- **¼ teaspoon ground nutmeg**
- **1 vanilla bean**
- **½ tablespoon sugar**
- **1 egg**
- **whipped cream, cocoa, cinnamon sticks and marshmallows to garnish**

Place the chopped chocolate in a large saucepan and pour ¼ cup (60 ml) of boiling water over it. Stir until most of the chocolate is melted then, over low heat, add the milk and cream, stirring until the mixture is warm. Add the spices, vanilla and sugar and increase the heat. Whisk until the mixture starts to boil, then reduce the heat and simmer for 5 minutes, whisking continuously. Remove the saucepan from the heat.

In a bowl or mixer, whisk the egg until frothy. Gradually add a cup of the hot chocolate, whisking as you pour. Once combined, pour the mixture back into the saucepan and place over low heat. Whisk for 3 minutes.

Pour into warmed mugs and pipe whipped cream into each mug. Garnish with sifted cocoa, a cinnamon stick and marshmallows.

This is a surprisingly simple cake to make, and it's gluten-free!

Pistachio & almond cake with cardamom-laced citrus syrup

SERVES 6–8, GLUTEN-FREE

1 cup (200 g) raw sugar

3 cups (250 g) ground almonds

¾ cup (75 g) chopped pistachios

9 tablespoons (125 g) butter, melted

2 eggs, lightly beaten

1 cup (240 g) Greek-style yogurt

1 teaspoon ground nutmeg

½ teaspoon ground cinnamon

CITRUS SYRUP

2 oranges

1–2 lemons

1 cup (200 g) sugar

2 cinnamon sticks

2–3 cardamom pods, crushed

Greek-style yogurt to serve

Preheat the oven to 325°F (160°C). Grease a 9–9½ in (22–24 cm) springform cake pan and line it with parchment paper.

In a large bowl, combine the sugar, ground almonds and ½ cup (50 g) of the chopped pistachios. Add the butter and stir until combined. Transfer half of the mixture to the prepared pan, pressing it down on the bottom.

Add the eggs, yogurt and spices to the remaining mixture. Mix well, then pour on top of the batter already in the pan. Sprinkle with the remaining pistachios.

Bake for 50–60 minutes or until a skewer inserted into the center of the cake comes out clean. Remove from the oven and set aside while you make the syrup.

To make the syrup, use a zester to peel long, thin strips of rind from half an orange. Squeeze the oranges to get ½ cup (120 ml) of juice. Squeeze the lemon/s to get ¼ cup (60 ml) of juice.

Place all citrus juices, orange rind strips, sugar, cinnamon sticks and cardamom pods into a saucepan. Stir over low heat until the sugar has dissolved. Bring to a gentle boil, then simmer, uncovered, for about 20 minutes until syrupy.

Drizzle ½ cup (120 ml) of the hot syrup over the warm cake, still in the cake pan, then let stand for 10 minutes before transferring to a plate. Decorate with the cinnamon sticks and a drizzle of the remaining warm syrup and serve with a dollop of yogurt.

These fried pastry cookies are so delicious, plus they are fun to make with your kids. When I was young we often had them after school. During the school break, Mom would let us help her make them as a treat.

Sakar para

MAKES 30–40

1 cup (250 ml) milk

1 cup (200 g) sugar

4 cups (500 g) all-purpose flour

½ cup (120 ml) ghee

1½ cups (350 ml) vegetable oil for frying

confectioners' sugar for dusting

In a saucepan, heat the milk and sugar until the sugar dissolves and the mixture is boiling, being careful it doesn't burn. Set aside to cool.

Sift the flour into a large bowl and add the ghee. Rub it in, making sure it's all combined. Add the cooled sweetened milk and mix into a dough.

Turn out the dough onto a floured surface and roll out to about ⅛ in (5 mm) thick.

In a deep pan, heat the vegetable oil to 350-375°F (180-190°C).

Cut the dough into diamond shapes, 2–2½ in (5–6 cm) in length. Fry in batches until golden. Place the cooked pastries on paper towels to absorb any excess oil.

Once cooled, dust with confectioners' sugar and enjoy. These are best eaten the same day.

This is a lovely way to use tamarillos. Served in shot glasses, it makes a lusciously creamy dessert with a little tartness that offsets the cream.

Tamarillo fool

SERVES 6–8

8 tamarillos, halved (see page 93)
½ cup (100 g) brown sugar
¼ teaspoon ground cinnamon
zest and juice of 1 orange
⅔ cup (150 ml) cream
1 cup (250 ml) Greek-style yogurt
2 tablespoons honey

Scoop the tamarillo flesh into a small saucepan with the sugar, cinnamon and orange zest and juice. Bring to a boil over medium heat, then reduce and simmer for 5 minutes until flesh is pulpy. Remove from heat and push through a sieve, reserving flesh. Return the juice to the saucepan and simmer for 6–8 minutes until reduced by half.

In a bowl, mash the reserved flesh and then pour the reduced syrup over it. Set aside to cool.

Whip the cream until soft peaks form, then fold in the yogurt and honey. Gently swirl in the tamarillo mixture, to create a marbled effect. Spoon the mixture into glasses, cover and refrigerate until ready to serve.

Here's an easy brioche dough recipe. It needs 24 hours in the fridge before baking so is best made the day before. It features my two favorite spices, cinnamon and cardamom—and the orange glaze makes these buns absolutely delectable.

Cardamom & cinnamon buns with orange glaze

MAKES 12

BRIOCHE DOUGH

3 cups (360 g) bread flour

1½ teaspoons instant yeast

⅓ cup (70 g) sugar

¾ teaspoon ground cardamom

¼ teaspoon ground cinnamon

¼ teaspoon salt

2 eggs

1 cup (250 ml) warm milk

1 teaspoon vanilla extract

7 tablespoons (125 g) butter, softened

FILLING

½ cup (100 g) sugar

1 teaspoon ground cardamom

1 teaspoon ground cinnamon

1 teaspoon orange zest

6 tablespoons (85 g) soft butter

ORANGE GLAZE

1 teaspoon finely grated orange zest

2 tablespoons warmed orange juice

1 cup (115 g) confectioners' sugar

handful of freeze-dried raspberries (optional)

In a bowl or mixer, combine the flour, yeast, sugar, spices and salt and mix. In a separate bowl, whisk together the eggs, milk and vanilla and pour this into the dry ingredients. Using an electric mixer or whisk, mix to combine. Gradually mix in the butter until you have a soft, sticky dough. Set aside to rise for a couple of hours (I leave it in the bowl of my mixer) and then transfer it to the fridge, covered, for 24 hours.

Preheat the oven to 350°F (180°C). Line a muffin pan with paper liners or a large cake pan with parchment paper.

Roll out the dough to form a 10 x 14 in (25 x 35 cm) rectangle.

Mix together the filling ingredients to form a paste and spread on top of the dough. Roll up the dough, starting from the longest side as if you were making a swiss roll. Using a sharp knife, cut the roll into 12 equal slices. Place the slices in the prepared pan. Bake for 25 minutes or until risen and a golden color.

To make the glaze, combine the orange zest and juice with the confectioners' sugar until you have a drizzle consistency (add a little extra orange juice if needed). Pour over the buns. The glaze will harden as it cools to give extra crunch. Sprinkle with the raspberries if using. These are best eaten on the day they are baked.

I couldn't have published a book of sweet things without including a traditional apple pie recipe. It's my Mom's favorite dessert, as well as mine, and uses spices that work beautifully with apples. It's best served with plenty of cream. This recipe makes a double-crust 9 in (23 cm) apple pie.

Old-fashioned apple pie

SERVES 8–10

- **14 oz (400 g) block of puff pastry, thawed, cut in half**
- **8–10 Granny Smith apples, peeled, cored and chopped***
- **2 tablespoons all-purpose flour**
- **¾ cup (150 g) white sugar**
- **1 teaspoon ground cinnamon**
- **½ teaspoon ground nutmeg****
- **½ teaspoon ground cloves**
- **½ teaspoon salt**
- **1 tablespoon lemon juice**
- **1 tablespoon finely grated lemon zest**
- **1 tablespoon butter, melted**
- **1 egg, beaten**
- **1 tablespoon raw sugar**
- **whipped cream or ice cream to serve**

Heat the oven to 350°F (180°C). Grease a 9 in (23 cm) pie dish.

On a lightly floured surface, separately roll out each pastry half to a circle about ¾ in (2 cm) larger in diameter than the prepared pie dish (they should be about ⅛ in/5 mm thick). Place one circle in the dish, cutting off any overlap, and the other on a baking sheet. Set aside in the refrigerator.

In a large bowl, toss together the chopped apples, flour, sugar, spices, salt, lemon juice and zest, and melted butter until combined. Transfer the coated apples to the chilled pie dish and arrange so they are evenly distributed. Pour any remaining liquid left in the bowl over the apples.

Top with the other dough circle. Fold the edges of the pastry together and turn it under the edge of the pie and crimp. Cut an X-shaped vent into the top and use any leftover pastry to make leaf shapes to decorate.

Refrigerate the uncooked pie for 15 minutes, then brush with beaten egg and sprinkle with the raw sugar.

Bake for 50–55 minutes until golden. Remove the pie from the oven and set aside to rest for 20 minutes before cutting.

Serve with your choice of whipped cream or ice cream.

* Granny Smiths work best but feel free to use a mixture of varieties.

** Freshly grated, if you happpen to have a whole nutmeg.

This gorgeous cake, oozing with buttery flavor, can be made gluten-free. It can be made ahead of time and reheated. Serve it with ice cream.

Sticky date cake with caramel sauce

SERVES 6

6 oz (170 g) Medjool dates, pitted and chopped
½ teaspoon vanilla extract
2 teaspoons hot chocolate powder
¾ teaspoon baking soda
7 tbsp (100 g) butter, softened
¾ cup (150 g) sugar (preferably superfine)
2 eggs, lightly beaten
1⅓ cups (170 g) self-rising flour (or use a gluten-free flour)

CARAMEL SAUCE

8 tbsp (120 g) butter
scant 1 cup (170 g) light brown sugar
6 tablespoons (90 ml) heavy cream

Preheat the oven to 325°F (160°C). Grease a 7 x 9 in (18 x 23 cm) baking dish.

In a bowl, pour ¾ cup (170 ml) boiling water over the dates. Add the vanilla, hot chocolate powder, and baking soda and leave to soak for 30 minutes or until the dates have soaked up most of the liquid.

In a large bowl or mixer, whisk the butter and sugar until pale and fluffy. Add the beaten eggs, sift in the flour and stir until well combined. Fold in the softened dates. Pour into the prepared dish and bake for 35–40 minutes or until a skewer inserted into the center comes out clean.

To make the sauce, gently heat the butter, sugar and cream in a saucepan until the sugar has dissolved. Bring to a simmer, then increase the heat and keep stirring until the contents take on a luscious caramel color.

Serve in bowls or cut into squares, with the caramel sauce poured over.

As you will probably have gathered by now, I love using fresh fruit in cakes and loaves and this gorgeous cake is no exception, It will send aromas of cinnamon wafting through your kitchen. It's delicious when served straight out of the oven, with slices slathered in butter. A perfect winter afternoon treat.

Spiced date, orange & apple loaf

SERVES 6–8

9 tbsp (125 g) butter
1 cup (240 ml) fresh orange juice
1 teaspoon baking soda
1 teaspoon ground cinnamon
¼ teaspoon freshly grated nutmeg
1 cup (200 g) brown sugar
2 apples peeled, cored and finely chopped
4 Medjool dates, pitted and chopped
2 eggs, beaten
1½ cups (190 g) self-rising flour, sifted
1 cup (115 g) rolled oats

Preheat the oven to 375°F (190°C). Line a 9½ x 4 in (24 x 11 cm) loaf pan.

Place the butter, orange juice, baking soda, spices, brown sugar, apples and dates in a large pot over medium heat and bring to a boil. Reduce the heat and allow it to simmer, stirring occasionally, for about 5 minutes. Remove from the heat and set aside to cool for 15–20 minutes.

Fold the beaten eggs into the cooled apple mixture, followed by the flour and the rolled oats. Pour the mixture into the prepared pan and bake for 30–40 minutes until golden and cracks appear on the top.

Serve warm, with lots of butter.

The rich flavor of gingerbread is so inviting, and the combined aromas of the spices used in this cake make it a wonderful treat any time of year. I've included it in this chapter because I think serving it warmed with a rich caramel sauce makes the perfect winter dessert. This recipe makes one large loaf or two small ones or a 9 in (22 cm) round cake.

Gingerbread cake with caramel sauce

SERVES 8–10

2 cups (250 g) all-purpose flour
1 teaspoon baking soda
1 teaspoon baking powder
1 cup (200 g) brown sugar
1½ tablespoons ground ginger
½ teaspoon ground nutmeg
¼ teaspoon ground cardamom
1 teaspoon ground cinnamon
2 sticks (225 g) butter
1⅓ cups (475 g) golden syrup (or light molasses)
2 eggs, lightly beaten
1 cup (250 ml) milk

CARAMEL SAUCE

1 stick (120 g) salted butter
170g brown sugar
6 tablespoons (90 ml) heavy cream

SALTED CARAMEL SHARDS

1 cup (200 g) sugar
1 tablespoon sea salt flakes

Preheat the oven to 300°F (150°C). Grease your preferred pan/s.

In a large bowl, sift the flour, baking soda and baking powder and add the brown sugar and spices.

In a small saucepan, heat the butter and golden syrup (or molasses) over low heat until melted, then add to the dry ingredients. Whisk in the eggs and milk. The mixture will be runny; that's okay. Pour into the prepared pan/s and bake for about 1 hour 10 minutes or until a skewer inserted into the center comes out clean.

For the sauce, gently melt the butter, sugar and cream in a saucepan until the sugar has dissolved. Bring to a simmer. Keep stirring, increase the heat to bring to a boil until the sauce is thick and luscious. Remove from the heat.

To make the shards, place the sugar and ¼ cup (60 ml) of water in a saucepan over low heat to dissolve the sugar. Turn up the heat and swirl the pan until the contents turn a light golden color, about 4 minutes. Pour onto a foil-lined pan and sprinkle with the salt. Set aside to cool, then break into shards when completely cool and hard.

Serve with a good drizzle of the sauce and decorated with the shards.

This is a decadent Indian bread pudding. Of Mughlai origin, it is traditionally made with ghee and is sweetened with condensed milk and spices, then garnished with nuts. It's rich and comforting—and reminds me of my childhood.

Shahi Tukra

SERVES 6–8

- **10 slices brioche (or any white bread)**
- **2½ cups (600 ml) milk**
- **1 cup (250 ml) sweetened condensed milk**
- **4–5 cardamom pods**
- **small cinnamon stick, ¾–1 in (2–3 cm)**
- **pinch of saffron (optional)**
- **1½ cups (150 g) mascarpone**
- **2–3 tablespoons ghee or butter**
- **4 tablespoons chopped nuts (e.g. pistachios, almonds)**
- **¼ cup (40 g) raisins or golden raisins**
- **2 tablespoons sugar plus ¼ teaspoon cinnamon, mixed together**
- **rose petals, sliced pistachios and edible gold dust to garnish (optional)**
- **whipped cream or ice cream to serve**

Preheat the oven to 350°F (180°C). Grease a 9 x 13 in (23 x 33 cm) baking dish with butter.

Cut off the crusts of the bread and cut each slice into two triangles.

In a large heavy-based pot, mix together the milk, condensed milk, cardamom, cinnamon and saffron, if using. Bring to a boil over medium–low heat, add the mascarpone and, using a wooden spoon, stir until smooth. Cook over low heat until thick, then remove from the heat and set aside.

In a frying pan, heat the ghee and fry the bread triangles until golden on both sides. Arrange the bread slices in the prepared baking dish so that they slightly overlap each other. Pour the mascarpone mixture over the slices and sprinkle with nuts, raisins and cinnamon sugar. Bake for 15–20 minutes until golden.

Scatter with rose petals, pistachios and gold dust if using and serve with a dollop of whipped cream or ice cream.

These little cakes are perfect to serve at a party. The sharpness of the rhubarb mixed with the delicate rose water makes a delicious combination. You can use fresh or frozen rhubarb in this recipe.

Vanilla, rose & rhubarb cupcakes

MAKES 12

- **9 tablespoons (125 g) softened butter, plus extra for greasing**
- **4 oz (120 g) rhubarb, washed, drained and chopped into ½ in (1 cm) pieces**
- **1 tablespoon brown sugar**
- **generous ½ cup (125 g) sugar (preferably superfine)**
- **1 cup (125 g) self-rising flour, sifted**
- **1 teaspoon baking powder**
- **2 eggs**
- **seeds of 1 vanilla bean, or 1 teaspoon vanilla paste**

ROSE WATER BUTTERCREAM

- **7 tablespoons (100 g) butter, softened**
- **¼ cup (60 ml) milk**
- **½ tablespoon vanilla extract**
- **4 cups (450 g) confectioners' sugar, sifted**
- **4–6 drops rose water**
- **dried edible dried rose petals and silver sugar pearls to decorate (optional)**

Preheat the oven to 375°F (190°C). Line a 12-hole muffin pan with paper cupcake liners.

In a small pot, cook the rhubarb and brown sugar over low heat for 5 minutes. Leave to cool.

In a large bowl, combine the butter, sugar, flour, baking powder, eggs and vanilla and beat until well combined. Add the chopped rhubarb to the mixture and stir to gently combine.

Spoon the mixture into the prepared pan and bake for 18–20 minutes until golden. Remove from the oven and place tray on a wire rack to cool.

To make the frosting, whisk the butter with an electric mixer for 1–2 minutes. Add the milk, vanilla and half of the confectioners' sugar and whisk for 3–4 minutes or until light and fluffy. Add the remaining confectioners' sugar, along with the rose water, and whisk for a further 3–4 minutes until spreadable. Add extra milk if the mixture is too dry or a bit more confectioners' sugar if it is too wet.

Spread or pipe the frosting onto the cakes and decorate with dried rose petals and silver sugar pearls if desired.

Quite a mouthful, I know, but I wanted the name to entice you into making this easy brownie that you can serve in the skillet. Topped with ice cream, this is a chocolatey, gooey dessert that you will love sharing.

Chocolate & peanut butter skillet brownie

SERVES 6

14 tablespoons (200 g) butter
7 oz (200 g) dark chocolate
7 oz (200 g) brown sugar
3 eggs
scant 1 cup (100 g) flour, sifted
½ cup (50 g) unsweetened cocoa
¼ teaspoon baking powder
½ teaspoon ground cinnamon
pinch of salt
¾ cup (200 g) peanut butter
chocolate chips and roasted peanuts to garnish (optional)
ice cream to serve

Preheat the oven to 350°F (180°C).

Grease a cast-iron skillet, about 9½ in (24 cm) in diameter, with a little of the butter. Melt the remaining butter and chocolate in a large bowl set over a pot of gently simmering water, stirring until smooth.

Remove from the heat and add the sugar and the eggs to the chocolate, one at a time, mixing well between each addition. Stir in the flour, cocoa, baking powder, cinnamon and salt and mix to combine, but don't overmix.

Pour the batter into the skillet and use a spatula to spread it out evenly to the sides. Dollop spoonfuls of peanut butter onto the batter and use a knife to swirl it through.

Bake for 20–22 minutes or until it's set around the edges and has a slightly fudgy center. While still hot, decorate with chocolate chips and peanuts, if using. Serve warm with ice cream.

Essentially an upside-down tart made with flaky pastry and a gorgeous sticky caramel sauce, this takes a little time and patience to prepare (an ovenproof skillet/frying pan is essential). But when you get it right, it not only tastes divine, it looks pretty impressive, too. Star anise goes beautifully with pear and in this case gives a warming zing to the tart. However, you can also make this tart with apples, stone fruit or bananas.

Spiced pear tarte tatin

SERVES 8–10

5–6 pears

½ cup (100 g) sugar

4 tablespoons (60 g) butter, cubed

2–3 star anise

pinch of cinnamon

squeeze of lemon juice

8–10½ oz (245–300 g) puff pastry, thawed

vanilla ice cream or whipped cream to serve

Preheat the oven to 350°F (180°C).

Peel, core and quarter the pears.

Place the sugar in an ovenproof frying pan or skillet (large enough to accommodate the quartered pears in one layer; mine is 9 x 9 in/23 x 23 cm) and cook over medium heat until it starts to melt. Swirl the pan until the sugar becomes a lovely golden color, but don't be tempted to stir or it will crystallize.

Add the butter, and once melted add the star anise and the cinnamon. Place the pears in the pan, cut-side down, and add the squeeze of lemon. Cook gently for 8–10 minutes, then set aside.

Dust the pastry with flour and roll it out on a clean work surface to about ½ in (1 cm) in thickness. Cut out a circle that is about ¾ in (2 cm) larger in diameter than the pan or skillet.

Gently place the pastry circle on top of the pears and carefully tuck the edges in all around. Prick a few holes on the top, then bake for 20–25 minutes or until the pastry is lovely and golden. Cool in the pan for 10 minutes.

Place a large plate over the pan and carefully flip it over so that the tart is upside-down on the plate (i.e., the deliciously caramelized pears are on the top).

Serve hot with vanilla ice cream or whipped cream.

Cast-iron gem pans are no longer common, so if you are lucky enough to own one, look after it (I found mine in a secondhand shop). Really quick to make, these moist little morsels are perfect to serve with a cup of tea. If you don't have a cast-iron gem pan, you can use a friand pan or muffin pan.

Spiced gems with mandarin drizzle

MAKES 12

3 tablespoons butter, plus extra for greasing
¼ cup (50 g) sugar
1 teaspoon ground ginger
½ teaspoon ground cardamom
1 egg
2 tablespoons golden syrup (or light molasses)
1 cup (125 g) all-purpose flour
1 teaspoon baking soda
½ cup (120 ml) milk

MANDARIN DRIZZLE

1 cup (115 g) confectioners' sugar
pinch of ground cardamom
1–2 tablespoons mandarin juice, warmed
freeze-dried mandarin segments or whipped cream (optional)

Preheat a cast-iron gem pan by placing it in an oven set to 400°F (200°C).

In a large bowl or mixer, whisk the butter, sugar and spices until light and fluffy. Add the egg and whisk well. Add the golden syrup (or molasses) and whisk again. Sift the flour into the mixture. Dissolve the baking soda in the milk and stir into the mixture.

Generously grease the hot gem pan with butter and spoon the batter into the sizzling cups. Bake for 10 minutes or until risen and golden brown.

As soon as the gems are out of the oven and have cooled slightly, mix the confectioners' sugar and cardamom with the warmed mandarin juice until spreadable. Drizzle over the gems.

Serve with the mandarin drizzle and freeze-dried mandarin segments (if using) or split them and fill with whipped cream.

Spring

Emerging from the hibernation of winter, these recipes will bring the fresh, light air of spring to your baking with delicately scented rose and cardamom madeleines, glazed lemon and poppy seed cake and pistachio and lavender éclairs. As with the other chapters, this one is dedicated to helping you discover how spices can magically transform your baking and desserts into something quite beautiful.

"The magic in new beginnings is truly the most powerful of them all."
JOSIYAH MARTIN

Lavender has such a beautiful, calming scent. It makes a heavenly pairing with pistachios for these éclairs. My mom made all her own éclairs, choux buns, choux swans and cream horns when we were kids, so this is my homage to her French pastry prowess.

Pistachio & lavender éclairs with mascarpone

MAKES 14–16

4 tablespoons (60 g) butter

1 cup (120 g) all-purpose flour, sifted

3 large eggs, beaten

1½ cups (250 g) chocolate chips or melts, white, dark or milk

1 cup (250 g) mascarpone or whipped cream

¼ cup (30 g) finely ground pistachios, plus extra if desired

½ cup (65 g) food-grade lavender

Preheat the oven to 425°F (210°C). Line two baking sheets with parchment paper.

In a small pot, melt the butter and 1 cup (240 ml) of water over low heat. When the water starts to simmer, remove from the heat and add the flour. Return to the heat and beat with a wooden spoon until the mixture is glossy and forms a smooth ball. Set aside to cool for 5 minutes and then gradually add the beaten eggs.

Fit a pastry bag with a large tip (star or round), pipe the mixture onto the prepared pans in 4 x 1 in (10 x 3 cm) strips. Bake for 10 minutes, then reduce the heat to 350°F (180°C) and bake for a further 15–20 minutes until golden and dry.

Make a small slit in each éclair to allow the steam to escape. Let them cool and then cut each one lengthwise almost all the way through.

Microwave the chocolate in a microwave-safe bowl in 30-second bursts until thick and spreadable.

Mix together the mascarpone and ground pistachios and transfer to a pastry bag. Fill each éclair with mascarpone and then carefully dip the top of each éclair into the melted chocolate. Sprinkle with the lavender (and extra pistachios if desired).

This moist cake with its hint of spices complemented by the tartness of the raspberries offers it a fresh and vibrant flavor profile. Add to this the zing of citrus and it all comes together beautifully.

Orange, raspberry & pistachio cake

SERVES 8–10

1½ cups (190 g) all-purpose flour

2 teaspoons baking powder

½ teaspoon ground ginger

½ teaspoon ground cardamom

¾ teaspoon salt

1 cup (200 g) sugar

3 eggs

1½ cups (340 g) ricotta cheese

finely grated zest of 1 orange

2 tablespoons orange juice

1 teaspoon vanilla extract

½ cup (115 g) brown butter*

1 cup (130 g) raspberries, fresh or frozen

⅓ cup (35 g) chopped pistachios

yogurt to serve

CANDIED ORANGE SLICES

1½ cups (400 g) sugar

1–2 oranges, thinly sliced

sugar crystals (optional)

Make the candied orange slices ahead of time. In a saucepan, dissolve the sugar in 1½ cups (350 ml) of water over medium–low heat. Add the sliced oranges and simmer for 30–40 minutes or until they become translucent. Remove the slices from the pan and dry on a wire rack. Sprinkle with sugar crystals if desired or leave plain. Alternatively, if time is short, place orange slices on top of the cake before it goes in the oven.

Preheat the oven to 350°F (180°C). Grease and line a 9 in (23 cm) springform cake pan.

Sift the flour, baking powder, spices and salt into a bowl. Whisk in the sugar and set aside. In another bowl, whisk the eggs, ricotta, orange zest and juice and vanilla together.

Add the egg mixture to the dry ingredients and combine. Fold in the browned butter, then the raspberries (saving a few for the top of the cake).Pour the batter evenly into the prepared cake pan. Sprinkle the top with the pistachios and reserved raspberries. Sprinkle with more sugar crystals for a crunchy topping.

Bake for 50–60 minutes or until a skewer inserted into the center comes out clean. Decorate with the candied orange slices and serve with a dollop of yogurt.

* To brown butter, heat it in a saucepan over medium heat until it starts foaming, with light brown specks, and it starts to smell nutty. Remove from the heat and set aside until required.

These delicate, buttery French cakes are such a joy to eat. The cardamom gives them a lovely flavor and the icing and rose petals add a slightly exotic Eastern touch. It's not essential to ice them, instead just dust with a little confectioners' sugar. You will need a madeleine pan to achieve their classic scallop shell shape. Best eaten on the day they are made.

Rose & cardamom madeleines

MAKES 12

1 cup (125 g) all-purpose flour, sifted

½ teaspoon baking powder

¼ teaspoon ground cardamom

pinch of salt

3 large eggs

⅔ cup (130 g) sugar

1 vanilla bean or 1 teaspoon vanilla extract

4 tablespoons (60 g) butter, melted

TO DECORATE

1 cup (115 g) confectioners' sugar

crushed pistachios

edible dried rose petals

In a small bowl, whisk together the flour, baking powder, ground cardamom and salt until well combined. Using a stand mixer or handheld mixer, whisk the eggs and sugar at medium–high speed for 5 minutes. Add the vanilla and whisk briefly to combine.

Sift a small amount of the flour mixture into the egg mixture and fold it in gently. Add the remaining flour, again folding it in gently. Gradually drizzle the melted butter into the mixture, folding to combine.

Cover the bowl and refrigerate for at least 30 minutes, preferably longer, to firm up.

Preheat the oven to 375°F (195°C). Dust the madeleine pan with flour before dropping in tablespoons of the mixture into each of the molds. Bake for 10 minutes or until golden. Remove from the oven and set aside to cool.

To make the icing, beat together the confectioners' sugar and enough hot water to achieve a spreadable consistency. Dip the corners of each madeleine into the icing. Sprinkle with crushed pistachios and dried rose petals.

An Indian version of shortbread, these are buttery and crisp with a hint of spice and remind me of my childhood when Mom let us help form the balls. Every Indian family has their own version, some with eggs and some without.

Naan khathai with white chocolate drizzle & raspberries

MAKES ABOUT 24

¾ cup (g) confectioners' sugar
½ cup (125 g) softened ghee or butter
pinch of saffron (optional)
1 egg
½ cup (120 ml) neutral oil
2 cups (250 g) all-purpose flour, sifted
½ teaspoon ground cardamom
1 cup (170 g) white chocolate chips or melts
4 tablespoons freeze-dried raspberries

Preheat the oven to 325°F (160°C). Line two baking sheets with parchment paper.

In a stand mixer or bowl, whisk the sugar, ghee and saffron, if using, until light and fluffy. Add the egg and oil and continue to mix. Add the flour and cardamom and mix to form a soft dough. (If the dough is too soft, refrigerate for 15 minutes.)

Form small balls of dough (each about 1 tablespoon) and space them out on the lined pans. Press down on each ball with a fork (or roll out the dough and use a small cookie cutter if you prefer but I quite like them rustic).

Bake for 20–25 minutes or until pale golden. Cool on wire racks.

Place the chocolate in a heatproof container and microwave in 20-second bursts until melted. Drizzle chocolate onto the cookies while they are still on the wire racks (place a sheet of parchment paper underneath to catch the drips) and sprinkle the raspberries on top.

My twin sister Anjum developed this recipe, so of course it always reminds me of her. It's one she would make for her spring and summer barbecues, back when we all lived in the UK. Refreshing and tangy, it's easy to whip up and can be made the day before—just sprinkle it with grated chocolate an hour before serving.

Anj's lemon & ginger crunch pie

SERVES 6–8

7 oz (200 g) ginger cookies, finely crushed
5 tablespoons (75 g) butter, melted
generous 1 cup (280 ml) heavy cream
1 x 14 oz (400 g) can of sweetened condensed milk
finely grated zest and juice of 3 lemons
2 oz (60 g) milk chocolate, finely grated

Mix the crushed ginger cookies with the melted butter. Press the crumb mixture into an 8 in (20 cm) springform cake pan.

In a bowl or mixer, whisk the cream to peaks. In a separate bowl, mix the condensed milk with the lemon zest and juice. Add the whipped cream and mix until well combined.

Pour the lemon cream mixture onto the cookie base and use a knife to smooth the top. Sprinkle with grated chocolate and refrigerate for at least a couple of hours before serving.

Here is another easy-to-make yet divinely rich dessert that can be made vegan and dairy-free by using vegan chocolate and vegan condensed milk. Decorate with a dusting of cocoa and gold dust to really set it off.

Chocolate & cardamom mousse loaf

SERVES 8–10

½ cup (120 ml) sweetened condensed milk

1 cup (240 ml) almond milk

1 x 14 oz (400 ml) can full-cream coconut milk

2 teaspoons instant coffee mixed with ¼ cup (60 ml) hot water

¼ cup (40 g) coconut sugar

⅓ cup (30 g) unsweetened cocoa powder dissolved in ¼ cup (60 ml) hot water

½ teaspoon ground cardamom

2–3 whole cardamom pods, lightly crushed

1 teaspoon agar agar powder

5½ oz (150 g) dark chocolate, chopped

cocoa powder and edible gold leaf to decorate (optional)

Place the milks, coffee, sugar, cocoa mixture, and cardamoms in a pot and whisk until smooth. Bring to a boil over medium heat, then add the agar agar. Reduce the heat and stir until the grains are dissolved—this will take a couple of minutes. Keeping the pot over the heat, whisk in the chocolate until melted.

Strain the mixture into a mini loaf pan (mine is 3½ x 5 in/9 x 12 cm). Cool completely and then refrigerate, ideally overnight. Dust with cocoa and gold leaf before serving, if desired.

This recipe comes from a great food writer friend who has inspired me on my own food journey. Fragranced with nutmeg, rose and citrus, it is an absolute pleasure to eat.

Bernie's Armenian nutmeg cake

SERVES 8

1½ cups (180 g) all-purpose flour

2 teaspoons baking powder

1¼ cups (270 g) firmly packed brown sugar

½ cup (45 g) ground almonds

9 tbsp (125 g) butter

1 teaspoon baking soda

½ cup (120 ml) milk

½ cup (120 ml) plain yogurt

1 egg

1 teaspoon freshly grated nutmeg

finely grated zest of 1 orange

½ cup (50 g) chopped pistachios

2–3 drops rose water

honey to drizzle

edible dried rose petals to garnish (optional)

Preheat the oven to 350°F (180°C). Grease and line the bottom of an 8 in (20 cm) springform cake pan.

Sift the flour and baking powder into a large bowl and mix in the brown sugar and ground almonds. Using your fingers, rub the butter into the mixture until it resembles breadcrumbs.

Press one-third of this mixture into the bottom of the prepared pan.

In a separate bowl, mix the baking soda with the milk. Whisk in the yogurt, egg, nutmeg and orange zest. Fold into the remaining flour mixture, ensuring it is well combined.

Pour the batter over the dough base in the pan. Sprinkle with the chopped pistachios and bake for 40–50 minutes or until a skewer inserted in the center comes out clean.

Remove from the oven and allow the cake to cool before turning out.

Mix the rose water with the honey and drizzle over the cake. Decorate with rose petals if desired.

These little tarts are so delectable—and a hint of pink peppercorns just elevates this dessert. Serve with runny cream or ice cream, or drizzle with caramel sauce.

Spiced banana tarts

SERVES 4

2–3 sheets puff pastry

2 very ripe bananas

1 cup (85 g) freshly grated or desiccated coconut

4 ripe bananas, peeled

½ teaspoon pink peppercorns

½ teaspoon black peppercorns

7 tablespoons (100 g) butter, melted

2 tablespoons raw sugar

caramel sauce (page 114) to serve, optional

whipped cream to serve

Preheat the oven to 400°F (200°C). Line a baking sheet with parchment paper.

Place the pastry sheets on a lightly floured surface and cut out four 4 in (10 cm) rounds. Place on the lined baking sheet and set aside.

Peel and mash the first two bananas with the coconut and spread over each of the pastry rounds.

Slice the four remaining bananas into 1 in (3 cm)-thick angled slices and place a few on top of each mashed banana and coconut-topped pastry.

Crush all the peppercorns in a mortar and pestle.

Brush each pastry all over with the melted butter (retain some butter for later), then sprinkle with the crushed peppercorns and raw sugar.

Bake for 25 minutes or until the pastry is golden and the bananas are caramelized. Remove from the oven, brush with the remaining butter and bake for another 2–3 minutes.

Serve hot, drizzled with caramel sauce, if using, with a dollop of whipped cream.

These chewy Italian-style cookies originate in Siena and are traditionally served at Christmastime. This version is from my food writer and stylist friend Bernie.

Tuscan Ricciarelli cookies

MAKES 18

2 egg whites
¼ cup (60 g) confectioners' sugar, plus extra for rolling
2 cups (160 g) ground almonds
⅔ cup (120 g) superfine sugar
finely grated zest of 1 orange or lemon
1 vanilla bean, seeds scraped, or 1 teaspoon vanilla extract

In a bowl or stand mixer, whisk the egg whites and confectioners' sugar until stiff peaks form. In a separate bowl, combine the ground almonds, superfine sugar, zest and vanilla. Fold the almond mixture into the egg whites to form a stiff dough. Refrigerate for at least 1 hour (the longer the better).

Preheat the oven to 325°F (170°C). Line two baking sheets with parchment paper.

Dust your work surface with the extra confectioners' sugar, then turn out the dough. Roll the dough in the sugar to prevent it from getting too sticky. Break off small walnut-sized pieces and roll each piece into a small log, then gently roll in a bit more confectioners' sugar. Place on the lined pans, allowing 2 in (5 cm) between each log. Gently press each one with two fingers to create a couple of indents, then dust with more confectioners' sugar. Set aside to rest at room temperature for 15 minutes.

Bake the cookies for 8–10 minutes or until light golden and slightly cracked. Remove from the oven and cool before serving.

This luscious no-churn ice cream, with its delicate flavors, keeps well in the freezer, making it a great dessert to bring out when unexpected visitors arrive.

Lavender, orange-blossom & honey ice cream

SERVES 6–8

1 tablespoon food-grade lavender

2 tablespoons confectioners' sugar

¼ cup (120 ml) honey

½ cups (375 ml) heavy cream

2–3 drops orange blossom water

zest of 1 small orange

⅓ cup (80 ml) whole milk

crystallized lavender sprigs (optional)*

Grind the lavender and confectioners' sugar in a mortar and pestle until fine. Warm the honey in the microwave for 10 seconds until very runny.

In a bowl or stand mixer, whisk the cream into soft peaks, taking care not to over-whip. Fold in the lavender sugar, honey, cream, orange blossom water, zest, and milk. Spoon the mixture into a shallow metal container, then cover and freeze until firm.

Remove the ice cream from the freezer 20 minutes before serving. Garnish with the crystallized lavender sprigs if desired.

* To crystallize the lavendar sprigs, brush a few lavender sprigs with beaten egg white and then dip in sugar. Set aside in a dry place overnight.

These delightful little cakes, adapted from a recipe by my friend Bernie, are ideal to make for a celebration but casual enough for a picnic. They feature a perfect pairing of chocolate and culinary lavender and because they freeze well, they are handy if you suddenly need a small cake to surprise someone. Best removed from the freezer the night before you need them.

Chocolate & lavender baby cakes

MAKES 6

5½ oz (150 g) dark chocolate, at least 60% cocoa, broken into small pieces
18 tablespoons (250 g) butter, softened
1¾ cups (350 g) sugar (preferably superfine)
4 eggs
2 cups (250 g) all-purpose flour
⅓ cup (30 g) cocoa powder
1 teaspoon baking soda
1 teaspoon vanilla extract
2 teaspoons food-grade lavender
1 cup (240 ml) buttermilk
frosted lavender (optional)*

CHOCOLATE FROSTING

10½ oz (300 g) dark chocolate, chopped into small pieces
¾ cup (170 ml) heavy cream
3 tablespoons butter

Heat the oven to 375°F (190°C). Grease and line the bottoms of six 4 in (10 cm) cake pans.

Combine the chocolate and ½ cup (120 ml) of hot water in a bowl set over a pot of simmering water and stir until the chocolate is melted. Remove from the heat and set aside.

In a bowl or stand mixer, whisk the butter and sugar until light and fluffy. Add the eggs, one at a time, whisking well after each addition.

Sift the flour, cocoa and baking soda into the chocolate and fold the chocolate mixture into the butter and sugar mixture. Add the vanilla, lavender and buttermilk and mix gently until combined.

Divide the mixture among the prepared pans and bake for 45 minutes or until a skewer inserted into the center of one comes out clean. Allow the cakes to cool in their pans before turning out.

To make the chocolate frosting, combine the chocolate, cream and butter in a bowl, set over a saucepan of simmering water and stir until melted and smooth. Remove from the heat and set aside to cool and thicken.

Spread frosting over the cakes when they are completely cool and garnish with frosted lavender.

*To make frosted lavender, brush with a little beaten egg white and sprinkle with sugar.

I love making this beautiful sorbet packed full of gorgeous flavors. The inclusion of basil seeds, which are used in Ayurvedic medicine and have a number of health benefits, gives it a little crunch. Iron and calcium-rich, basil seeds can also be used in drinks, ice creams and even cakes.

Berry, basil seed & lemon sorbet

SERVES 6–8, GLUTEN-FREE

1 cup (200 g) sugar

1 cup (20 g) lightly packed fresh basil leaves

6 cups (900 g) berries of your choice, fresh or frozen

¾ cup (170 ml) lemon juice (about 4 lemons)

1 tablespoon basil seeds

In a pot over high heat, combine the sugar with 1 cup (240 ml) of water, stirring occasionally, until the sugar has dissolved. Add the basil, remove from the heat and then cover the pot. Let stand for 15–20 minutes. Strain into a bowl, discard the leaves and refrigerate until cold.

Transfer the chilled liquid to a blender and add the berries and lemon juice. Blend until smooth. Add the basil seeds and mix to combine.

Scrape the mixture into an 8 in (20 cm) square or similar sized baking pan. Cover with plastic wrap and freeze until firm enough to scoop out spoonfuls to serve, about 2 hours. If it's frozen solid, allow it to thaw slightly before serving.

Another easy dessert or after-dinner treat, this recipe is very flexible—you can substitute any combination of dried fruit and nuts that you like. Chocolate and orange always go well together and the inclusion of a few spices adds extra flavor.

Orange, chile & chocolate bark

SERVES 10–12

¼ teaspoon ground cloves

4–6 cardamom pods, seeds removed and ground

¼ teaspoon cayenne pepper

¼ teaspoon ground chile

½ teaspoon ground cinnamon

14 oz (400 g) dark chocolate

⅔ cup (80 g) pistachios, coarsely chopped, plus extra to decorate

⅔ cup (80 g) cashews, coarsely chopped, plus extra to decorate

½ cup (60 g) dried cranberries, coarsely chopped, plus extra to decorate

finely grated zest of 1 orange

edible gold leaf flakes or luster dust (optional)

Line a baking sheet with parchment paper.

Place the spices in a small frying pan over medium heat. Allow them to toast without burning to release their aromas, 30–40 seconds. Remove from the heat and set aside.

Melt the chocolate, either in the microwave in short bursts (remove and stir every 30–40 seconds) or in a bowl set over a pot of simmering water.

Add the spices, nuts, cranberries and half of the orange zest to the melted chocolate and stir to combine. Pour onto the prepared pan, spreading it evenly. Scatter over the extra nuts and cranberries and the remaining orange zest and dust or sprinkle with edible gold if using.

Place in the fridge to set. Break into shards before serving.

This is such an easy dessert to whip up with leftover croissants. The result is a decadent bread pudding, with a hint of cardamom to give it a touch of the East.

Chocolate & cardamom ribbon croissant pudding

SERVES 10–12

cooking spray, for greasing

6 eggs

2⅓ cups (550 ml) heavy cream

⅔ cup (140 g) sugar, plus 2 tablespoons

1 tablespoon vanilla extract

¼ teaspoon ground cardamom

10½ oz (300 g) croissants, cut into 1 in (2.5 cm) chunks

3½ oz (100 g) chocolate (70% cocoa), chopped

melted chocolate to decorate

ice cream to serve (optional)

Preheat the oven to 350°F (180°C). Lightly grease a baking dish (I use an 11 in/28 cm round one) and set aside.

In a bowl, whisk together the eggs, heavy cream, ⅔ cup (140 g) of sugar, vanilla and cardamom.

Place half of the croissant chunks in the base of the baking dish. Scatter with the chopped chocolate and top with the remaining croissant chunks. Pour the egg mixture evenly over the croissants, scraping all of the mixture into the baking dish. Let it stand for 10 minutes. Sprinkle with the remaining 2 tablespoons of sugar, which will give it a lovely crunch.

Bake for 30–35 minutes or until the top is deeply golden in color and the mixture is set in the center. Remove from the oven and set aside to cool slightly.

Drizzle with extra melted chocolate and serve with ice cream or on its own.

A gorgeous cake to make in spring when you're craving sunny flavors. Use frozen or fresh blueberries, depending on availability.

Orange & blueberry bundt cake with clove syrup

SERVES 8–10

2 sticks (225 g) butter, softened, plus extra for greasing
1½ cups (300 g) sugar (preferably superfine)
4 eggs, separated
1 cup (225 g) plain yogurt
finely grated zest of 1 orange
⅓ cup (80 ml) freshly squeezed orange juice
2¼ cups (285 g) all-purpose flour
2 teaspoons baking powder
1 teaspoon baking soda
½ teaspoon salt
2 cups blueberries, fresh or frozen (don't thaw if frozen)

CLOVE SYRUP

¼ cup (60 ml) freshly squeezed orange juice
¼ cup (50 g) sugar
2 cloves
finely grated zest of 1 orange
whipped cream or yogurt to serve

Preheat the oven to 350°F (180°C). Grease and flour a large (9–10 in/23–25 cm) bundt pan.

In a large bowl, whisk the butter and sugar until light and fluffy. Add the egg yolks one at a time, whisking well after each addition. Mix in the yogurt, orange zest and juice.

In a separate bowl, sift the flour, baking powder and baking soda. In another bowl or your stand mixer, whisk the egg whites and salt until stiff peaks form. Fold the flour mixture into the butter mixture, then with a large metal spoon gradually fold in the egg whites. Finally, gently fold in the blueberries.

Pour the batter into the prepared pan. Bake for 50 minutes or until a skewer inserted into the center of the cake comes out clean.

In the last 15–20 minutes of baking, make the clove syrup. In a small saucepan combine the orange juice, sugar and cloves. Set over medium heat and stir until the sugar is dissolved.

Remove the cake from the oven. Place it on a wire rack and poke the top of the cake with a skewer. Remove the cloves from the syrup, brush half of the syrup over the cake, then leave to cool in the pan for 15 minutes. Turn out the cake and drizzle with the remaining syrup. Garnish with the orange zest and allow to cool completely.

Serve with a dollop of whipped cream or yogurt.

This recipe was shared with me by my friend Jo, whom I met when I first arrived in New Zealand. I was her daughter's nurse—that was 23 years ago. She originally made these for me when I had my firstborn, and I couldn't get enough of them. Full of oaty goodness, they were perfect for getting me through the early days of motherhood. You could try them with other dried fruits, too.

Apricot, ginger & oat slice

MAKES 10–12 SLICES

- **7 tablespoons (100 g) butter**
- **1 tablespoon honey**
- **¼ cup (50 g) brown sugar**
- **¼ cup (50 g) white sugar**
- **2 cups (230 g) rolled oats**
- **½ cup (45 g) desiccated coconut**
- **½ cup (65 g) chopped dried apricots**
- **2–3 small pieces crystallized ginger, finely chopped**
- **1 teaspoon vanilla extract**

FROSTING

- **¼ cup (70 g) crunchy peanut butter**
- **½ cup (85 g) chocolate chips (dark or milk)**

Line a microwave-safe dish with parchment paper (I use a 6 x 10 in/15 x 25 cm dish).

In a small heatproof bowl, microwave the butter and honey for 1 minute.

In a large bowl, mix together the remaining ingredients except the vanilla. Stir in the melted butter mixture and vanilla and combine well.

Press the mixture into the lined dish and microwave on high for 3 minutes. Carefully remove (it will be hot) and set aside to cool.

In another bowl, microwave the peanut butter and chocolate chips on high in short bursts until the chocolate has melted. Stir to mix and then spread it onto the cooled oat mixture.

Refrigerate until completely cool, then cut into slices or squares. Best stored in the fridge.

A lovely spicy drink with a refreshing kick of lime and mint.

Spiced iced tea

SERVES 4–6

1 teaspoon whole cloves

1 whole cinnamon stick (2–3 cm)

3 tea bags (black tea)

3/4 cup orange juice

1/2 cup (100 g) sugar

juice of 1 lime

small handful of chopped mint

In a saucepan, combine 6 cups of water with the spices and tea bags and bring to a boil. Remove from the heat and set aside to steep for up to 8 minutes.

In another saucepan, heat the orange juice, sugar and lime juice until boiling. Strain the steeped tea into the orange juice mixture. Add the mint and refrigerate until well chilled. Serve over ice.

When life gives you lemons, make this gorgeously moist lemon drizzle cake with a lovely crunch. It's drizzled with lemon syrup, topped with a simple icing and decorated with candied lemon slices.

Lemon & poppy seed cake with candied lemon slices

SERVES 6–8

9 tablespoons (125 g) butter, softened

1 cup (200 g) sugar (preferably superfine)

2 eggs

1½ cups (190 g) self-rising flour, sifted

pinch of salt

½ cup (120 ml) milk

finely grated zest of 1 lemon

1 tablespoon poppy seeds

CANDIED LEMON SLICES

1 cup (200 g) sugar

2 small–medium lemons, thinly sliced

TOPPING

⅓ cup (80 ml) lemon juice

¼ cup (50 g) sugar (preferably superfine)

ICING

1 cup (115 g) confectioners' sugar

1–2 tablespoons hot water

Preheat the oven to 350°F (180°C). Grease a 9 in (23 cm) ring or loaf pan.

In a bowl or stand mixer, whisk the butter and sugar together until light and fluffy. Whisk in the eggs, one at a time, then the flour, salt and milk. Stir in the lemon zest and poppy seeds and mix well to combine.

Pour the batter into the prepared pan and bake for 45 minutes.

While the cake is baking, make the candied lemon slices. Heat 1 cup (240 ml) of water and the sugar in a saucepan until the sugar has dissolved, then add the lemon slices. Leave to simmer on low heat until the slices are translucent. Remove the slices with a slotted spoon and set aside to cool until required.

To make the topping, combine the lemon juice and sugar in a saucepan and stir over low heat until the sugar has dissolved. Pour the topping over the cake after it has been removed from the oven and is still hot. Cool the cake in the pan.

When the cake is completely cool, mix the confectioners' sugar and hot water to achieve a drizzling consistency. Turn out the cake onto a plate and drizzle with the icing. Decorate with the candied lemon slices.

Burfi is a delicious Indian sweet, essentially a milky, almost fudge-like, dessert that's served on special occasions. This is my Mom's burfi recipe, which brings back so many wonderful memories whenever I make it. It can be flavored and colored to your liking. I've used rose water and food coloring; however you can also leave those out and just decorate it with rose petals and pistachios if you prefer.

Zarina's rose burfi

MAKES 24–26 PIECES

5 cups (500 g) powdered whole milk
2 tablespoons ghee or very soft butter
scant 1 cup (200 ml) heavy cream
1¼ cups (250 g) sugar
drop of pink food coloring
1 teaspoon rose water
Persian tea roses/edible dried rose petals to garnish
chopped pistachios (optional)

In a large bowl, combine the powdered milk with the ghee and cream and rub it together until the mixture looks like fine breadcrumbs.

In a large pot, place ½ cup (120 ml) of water along with the sugar, food coloring and rose water and heat for 8–10 minutes until the sugar is completely dissolved and the consistency is syrupy but runny.

Remove from the heat and add the milk mixture to the pot. Using a wooden spoon, stir until the mixture comes together and is well combined.

Line a 7 x 9½ in (18 x 24 cm) baking pan with parchment paper and spread the mixture onto it. Decorate with rose petals, and pistachios if desired, then leave to set for 2–3 hours (refrigerate if the weather is hot and humid).

When set, cut into desired shapes. Keep leftovers in an airtight container in the fridge for up to one week.

These chocolate truffles make a great foodie gift or a special after-dinner treat. The rose water adds a lovely fragrance and pairs beautifully with cardamom.

White chocolate, rose water & cardamom truffles

MAKES ABOUT 30

10½ oz (300 g) white chocolate, chopped, plus 3½ oz (100 g) extra to decorate
½ cup (120 ml) heavy cream
2 tablespoons unsalted butter
¼ teaspoon ground cardamom
½ teaspoon rose water
1 teaspoon vanilla paste
1 cup (100 g) desiccated coconut to coat (or use ground nuts, sprinkles or freeze-dried berries)

Line a baking sheet with parchment paper.

In a heatproof bowl set over a saucepan of just-simmering water, heat the chopped chocolate, cream and butter until melted. Alternatively, microwave this mixture in short bursts, stirring regularly, until melted and smooth. Stir in the cardamom, rose water and vanilla. Transfer to a shallow baking dish and refrigerate until set (best done overnight).

Using a large melon baller or a teaspoon, scoop out heaped teaspoons from the set mixture and roll into balls. Arrange the balls on the prepared pan and place in the freezer for 30 minutes.

For the decoration, chop and melt the remaining white chocolate using the method above, then leave to cool a little. Drop each truffle into the chocolate to coat, then lift with a fork or a toothpick and place on a wire rack to drain. Roll the truffles in desiccated coconut (or your preferred topping). Refrigerate until you are ready to serve.

"If more of us valued food and cheer and song above hoarded gold, it would be a merrier world."
J. R. R. TOLKIEN

Celebrations

For me, nothing beats a gathering of family and friends to celebrate a special occasion. The recipes in this chapter are for such occasions, whether it be a birthday, anniversary or some other kind of celebratory gathering. I've chosen these recipes to give you a selection of sublime desserts and cakes that have an extra "wow" factor. They may take a bit of time to create; however, I promise they're not too difficult, and the result will be so worth it.

Not only a pleasure to look at, this gorgeous cake is wonderfully decadent without being too rich—and it's actually not that difficult to make. If you want to make a three-layer cake, simply use smaller-sized cake pans, ideally 6½–7 in (16–18 cm).

Honey & banana cake

SERVES 8–10

12 tablespoons (160 g) butter, softened
¾ cup (160 g) brown sugar
⅓ cup (110 g) honey, plus extra for drizzling
finely grated zest of 2 lemons
4 very ripe bananas, mashed
3 eggs
2¾ cups (340 g) all-purpose flour
1½ teaspoons baking powder
1½ teaspoons baking soda
generous 1 cup (270 g) sour cream
1 tablespoon milk
3 ripe bananas, sliced to serve

HONEY FROSTING

1⅓ cups (300 g) cream cheese, at room temperature
⅔ cup (150 g) sour cream
3 tablespoons honey
seeds of 1 vanilla bean or 1 teaspoon vanilla paste or extract
finely grated zest of 1 lemon

CARAMEL DROPS

2 cups (400 g) sugar
6–8 hazelnuts
6–8 toothpicks

Preheat the oven to 325°F (170°C). Grease, flour and line the bottoms of two 9–9½ in (22–24 cm) cake pans.

Using a stand mixer or handheld mixer, beat the butter, brown sugar, honey and lemon zest until pale and fluffy. Stir in the mashed banana and eggs. Sift in the flour, baking powder and baking soda, and stir to combine. In a separate bowl, whisk together the sour cream and milk, then add to the banana mixture, stirring to combine. Divide the mixture between the cake pans, smoothing the tops.

Bake until the cakes are golden and spring back when lightly pressed, 35–40 minutes. Remove from the oven and cool the cakes in the pans for 10 minutes before turning out onto wire racks to cool completely.

For the frosting, whisk all of the ingredients together with an electric mixer until smooth.

To make the caramel drops, place the sugar in a saucepan over medium heat. Stir until melted and then remove from the heat. Insert a toothpick into each hazelnut. Dip in the warm caramel until coated. Hang the nuts over the edge of your kitchen counter (with something heavy on the toothpicks to stop them falling). The caramel will slowly drip and lengthen. Remove toothpicks once the caramel has hardened.

To assemble, spread one of the cakes with half of the frosting and scatter over the banana slices. Top with the remaining cake and spread with the remaining frosting. Drizzle with honey and add the caramel drops to serve.

This recipe was adapted from The Dairy Book of Home Cookery, *a book my family had in the UK back in the early 1990s. Choux pastry can be used for a variety of baked goods, including profiteroles and éclairs. This recipe can easily be halved.*

Cardamom & chocolate choux buns with saffron cream

MAKES 24 SMALL OR 12 LARGE

14 tablespoons (200 g) butter

2 cups (250 g) flour (sifted twice)

pinch of salt

8 eggs

1¼ cups (300 ml) heavy cream

pinch of saffron

CHOCOLATE FROSTING

1 tablespoon butter, melted

1 cup (115 g) confectioners' sugar, sifted

1 tablespoon cocoa

1–2 cardamom pods, seeds removed and crushed

edible gold dust (optional)

Preheat the oven to 400°F (200°C). Line a baking pan with parchment paper.

Place 1¼ cups (300 ml) of water and the butter in a pot. Heat on low until the butter melts, then bring to a brisk boil. Remove from the heat. Add the flour and salt and mix with a wooden spoon until it comes away from the sides of the pot and forms a soft ball. This will take 6–8 minutes. At this point you can transfer the dough to an electric mixer or continue to use your wooden spoon. Add the eggs, one at a time, and beat until the mixture is smooth and glossy and stands in soft peaks when lifted with a spoon.

Using an ice-cream scoop if you have one, scoop out 12 large or 24 small balls of dough, and arrange on the lined pan, leaving some space between them to give them room to rise in the oven. Bake for 20–25 minutes until nicely golden in color. Remove from the oven and set aside to cool.

Using an electric mixer, whisk the cream to soft peaks, then add the saffron and mix lightly. Set aside until required.

To make the frosting, melt the butter in a small saucepan over medium heat or in a microwave-safe bowl in the micowave. Add confectioners' sugar, cocoa, cardamom and enough boiling water (2–3 teaspoons) to make a thick, spreadable frosting.

When the buns are cool, cut each one almost in half and fill with cream (you can use a pastry bag or spoon). Drizzle the buns with chocolate icing and dust with gold dust for extra sparkle.

This take on the classic British Victoria sponge cake is adorned with whipped cream and jam of your choice, and topped with baked cherries glazed with maple syrup. For extra wow-factor, double the recipe to make four-tier cake like the one pictured (note that the following recipe is, however, for a two-layer cake).

Spiced Victoria sponge cake with maple-glazed cherries

SERVES 8–10

butter or cooking spray for greasing
¾ cup (100 g) all-purpose flour
½ cup (60 g) self-rising flour
½ teaspoon ground cinnamon
6 eggs
¾ cup (225 g) sugar (preferably superfine)
5 tablespoons (75 g) melted butter, cooled

FILLING

1 cup (250 ml) heavy cream
¾ cup (250 g) jam of your choice (I like raspberry or blackberry)

TOPPING

1 lb 5 oz (600 g) cherries with stems
2–3 tablespoons maple syrup
confectioners' sugar for dusting (optional)

Preheat the oven to 350°F (180°C). Grease two 8 in (20 cm) round cake pans.

Triple-sift the flours and cinnamon into a large bowl. This will make the cake light and fluffy.

Using a stand mixer or handheld mixer, whisk the sugar and eggs until pale and creamy (when you lift the whisk, it should form a ribbon).

Using a metal spoon, gently fold the sifted dry ingredients, about ¼ cup (30 g) at a time, into the egg mixture, until incorporated. Then fold in the melted butter. Divide between the prepared pans.

Bake the cakes for about 18 minutes or until springy when touched. Turn them both out onto a parchment paper-lined wire rack to cool.

Turn down the oven to 325°F (160°C). While the cakes are cooling, prepare the cherries. Wash and dry them, leaving the stems on. Place the cherries on a baking pan and drizzle with the maple syrup. Bake for 20–25 minutes until softened and juicy. Remove from the oven and set aside to cool.

Whisk the cream until soft peaks form (you can sweeten the cream with a little confectioners' sugar if you wish, or leave it plain). Spread one of the cake layers with jam, followed by a layer of whipped cream. Place the other cake layer on top. Top with the baked cherries and dust with confectioners' sugar, if you like.

Apart from the chocolate drizzle and the optional chocolate and cardamom swirl, this easy gluten-free meringue recipe has just four ingredients. Decorated with nuts or dried fruit, it makes a show-stopper of a dessert.

Meringue stack with chocolate drizzle

MAKES 8–10, GLUTEN-FREE

MERINGUES

1½ cups (300 g) superfine sugar

whites of 5 large eggs

pinch of salt

½ teaspoon vanilla bean paste

CHOCOLATE DRIZZLE

1 tablespoon cocoa

1 cup (115 g) confectioners' sugar

1 tablespoon butter, melted

2 teaspoons boiling water

CHOCOLATE & CARDAMOM SWIRL

⅓ cup (50 g) chocolate melts

¼ teaspoon ground cardamom

Preheat the oven to 400°F (200°C).

Spread the sugar for the meringues on a baking pan and place in the oven for 5 minutes. Remove the pan and set aside briefly. Reduce the oven temperature to 225°F (110°C).

Using a stand mixer or handheld mixer, whisk the egg whites with the salt until frothy. Add the hot sugar and the vanilla, then whisk on medium–high speed for 7–8 minutes until the mixture is glossy and stands in peaks. Set the meringue mixture aside to cool completely.

To make the chocolate and cardamom swirl, melt the chocolate in the microwave in short bursts, stirring frequently, then stir in the cardamom. Let it cool slightly, then pour it over the cooled meringue mixture, taking care just to pour, not fold it through.

Line a baking sheet with parchment paper. Dip an ice-cream scoop or spoon into the mixture and scoop out 8–10 generous portions, placing well spaced on the lined pan.

Bake for 1 hour, then turn off the oven and allow the meringues to cool in the oven.

To make the drizzle, add the cocoa and confectioners' sugar to the melted butter and mix with the boiling water to achieve a drizzle consistency.

Assemble the meringues in a stack and drizzle them with the chocolate.

This fragrant and pretty cake takes me back to my childhood with its combination of rose water and cardamom. Make it in a fluted bundt pan to wow your guests.

Persian love cake

SERVES 8–10

14 tablespoons (200 g) butter, softened, plus extra for greasing
heaped 1 cup (225 g) sugar (preferably superfine)
4 eggs
zest and juice of 1 orange
2 teaspoons rose water
1¼ cups (150 g) all-purpose flour
2 teaspoons baking powder
½ teaspoon baking soda
½ teaspoon ground cardamom
2⅓ cups (200 g) ground almonds
3 tablespoons sour cream

ICING

1 cup (115 g) confectioners' sugar
1 tablespoon orange juice
½ teaspoon rose water
edible dried rose petals, orange zest and pistachios to decorate

Preheat the oven to 325°F (170°C). Grease a 10 inch (25 cm) bundt pan with butter, ensuring that all the indentations are well greased.

Using a stand mixer or handheld mixer, cream the butter and sugar until really pale, then add the eggs, one at a time, mixing well and scraping down the sides between each addition. Add the orange zest and juice and the rose water, and mix. Sift in the flour, baking powder, baking soda, cardamom, ground almonds and sour cream, and mix well. Spoon the mixture into the prepared pan.

Bake for 35–40 minutes or until the cake has risen and a skewer inserted into the center comes out clean. Leave in the pan for 10 minutes before turning out onto a wire rack to cool.

To make the icing, whisk together the confectioners' sugar and orange juice to make a thick, pourable consistency. Mix in the rose water. Drizzle the icing over the cake, then decorate with rose petals, orange zest and pistachios.

This flaky, layered pastry takes me right back to when Mom used to make batches of them, ready for an after-school treat. I don't know why they are called "banana" puris—they don't look or taste anything like bananas. They are also known as khaja puris and can be made sweet or savory. These puris can be stored in an airtight container for a couple of days, prior to dipping in syrup.

"Banana" puris with saffron & rose syrup

MAKES 12–14

- 2 cups (250 g) all-purpose flour, plus extra for rolling
- pinch of salt
- ½ teaspoon baking powder
- 4 tablespoons (60 g) ghee or butter
- few drops of lemon juice
- ⅔ cup (150 ml) ice-cold water, plus extra if needed
- neutral oil for frying
- shredded coconut or edible dried rose petals to decorate

FILLING

- ½–¾ cup (120–180 ml) melted ghee or butter
- cornstarch for sprinkling

SYRUP

- 1 cup (200 g) sugar
- few drops of rose water
- 2–3 cardamom pods, slightly crushed
- pinch of saffron

In a bowl, mix the flour, salt and baking powder. Rub in the ghee or butter until the mixture resembles breadcrumbs. Mix the lemon juice and the ice-cold water and mix into the flour to make a soft dough. Cover and set aside for 30 minutes.

Sprinkle flour on your work surface and divide the dough into eight portions. Roll each into a ball, then and roll out each ball into a large thin roti (circle).To make the filling, brush each roti with melted ghee and sprinkle with cornstarch. Place the rotis, one on top of the other, to make eight layers. Brush the top roti with some ghee and sprinkle with a little cornstarch.

Roll up the pile of layered rotis to make a swiss roll shape. Cut into eight equal-sized slices, slightly flattening each at an angle to show the layers. Lightly roll each slice with a rolling pin to flatten just a little.

Add enough oil to a pot so it is 2 in (5 cm) deep. Gently heat the oil to a temperature of about 350°F (180°C), or until a small piece of bread dropped into the oil turns golden in 1 minute. Fry the puri in batches until golden and crisp on both sides. Drain on paper towels.

To make the syrup, combine all the ingredients in a small saucepan with 1 cup (240 ml) of water and heat until the sugar has dissolved and a sticky syrup has formed. Dip each puri in the syrup and place on a wire rack. Dust with shredded coconut or rose petals and serve.

I love using fruit in cakes, and this combination of cardamom and pear with a hint of citrus is not only divine but it looks pretty spectacular, too.

Whole pear & cardamom cake

SERVES 8–10

3 cups (600 g) sugar
1 cinnamon stick
1 star anise
pinch of saffron
6 whole pears, peeled with stem left on
3 cups (375 g) all-purpose flour
½ teaspoon salt
1½ teaspoons baking powder
½ teaspoon ground cardamom
1½ cups (350 ml) milk
1 cup (125 ml) vegetable oil
3 extra-large eggs
2 tablespoons grated orange zest
1 teaspoon vanilla extract

CARDAMOM & ORANGE GLAZE

2 cups (225 g) confectioners' sugar
finely grated zest of 1 orange
½ cup (120 ml) slightly warmed fresh orange juice
¼ teaspoon ground cardamom

Greek-style yogurt or crème fraîche to serve

Preheat the oven to 375°F (190°C). Grease a loose-bottomed tube pan and dust with flour.

In a large pot, heat 1 cup (125 ml) of water, ½ cup (100 g) of the sugar, the cinnamon stick, star anise and saffron and bring to a boil. Add the pears, then cover and simmer for 5–8 minutes until just tender, and still holding their shape. Drain and cool.

Sift the flour, salt, baking powder and cardamom into a large bowl. Stir in the remaining 2½ cups (500 g) of sugar. Make a well in the middle and add the milk, oil, eggs, orange zest and vanilla. Mix until smooth, then pour into the prepared pan.

Pat the pears dry and place them, standing with stems upright, in the batter. If they flop over, poke a metal skewer through the top of two pears at a time to hold them in place. The skewer should be long enough to reach the other side of the pan to balance the two pears.

Bake for 1 hour–1 hour and 10 minutes, or until a skewer inserted into the cake comes out clean. Remove the cake from the oven and cool in the pan for 30 minutes. If you have used skewers, remove them at this point. Turn the cake out of the pan (you will almost certainly need an extra pair of hands to help you do this) and set aside to cool.

Meanwhile, make the glaze. In a bowl, mix all the ingredients together until smooth. When the cake is cool, drizzle with the glaze and serve with a dollop of Greek-style yogurt or crème fraîche.

This stunning three-layer cake, with its combination of moist chocolate cake and pistachio-studded cream, will stop friends and family in their tracks. For a smaller cake, halve the recipe and use two 8-9 in (20-22 cm) cake pans.

Chocolate, pistachio & rose cake

SERVES 10–12

- 2 cups (400 g) sugar
- 2 eggs
- 1 cup (240 ml) milk
- 5 tablespoons (50 g) unsweetened cocoa powder
- 14 tablespoons (200 g) butter, melted and cooled
- pinch of salt
- 2 teaspoons baking soda
- 2 teaspoons baking powder
- 2 teaspoons vanilla extract or paste
- 3 cups (375 g) all-purpose flour, sifted
- ⅔ cup (165 ml) boiling water

FROSTING

- 14 tablespoons (200 g) butter, softened
- ½ cup (120 ml) milk
- 1 teaspoon rose water
- 8 cups (900 g) confectioners' sugar, sifted
- pink and/or pale green food coloring
- 2–3 cups (200–300 g) chopped pistachios
- edible dried rose petals or buds

Preheat the oven to 300°F (150°C). Grease three 6 in (15 cm) cake pans.

In a large mixing bowl, add all of the ingredients for the cake in the order listed. First, add the water, then using a handheld mixer or whisk, mix until the batter is thick and glossy and slightly runny. Pour the batter into the prepared pans. Bake for 25–30 minutes or until a skewer inserted into the center of each cake comes out clean.

If you are making both colors, split the frosting ingredients in half to make two batches (I used green for the outside and pink for the layers). Whisk the butter for 1–2 minutes until creamy. Add the milk, rose water and gradually mix in the sifted confectioners' sugar. Whisk for at least 3 minutes or until the mixture is light, fluffy and a spreadable consistency. Add a little extra milk if it's too dry, or more confectioners' sugar if it's too wet. Add the food coloring, a small drop at a time, until you have your desired color(s).

Place the bottom layer of the cake on the plate or stand it will be served on. Spread the top with frosting and top with the next cake later. Repeat with the final layer, reserving enough frosting to completely cover the outside of the cake. Gently push handfuls of the chopped pistachios into the frosting so they stay in place—there is no easy way to do this but patience is key and the result is amazing. Finish it off by either studding the cake with dried rose buds or sprinkle with dried rose petals.

Here is another absolutely gorgeous dessert that's perfect for a special dinner party. Pink Lady apples are best as they work really well and pair well with the spiced cookies.

Spiced apple-blossom tart

SERVES 8

3 large Pink Lady or other apples, cored and thinly sliced
¼ cup (50 g) brown sugar
¼ cup (50 g) white sugar, plus 2 tablespoons
½ teaspoon ground cinnamon
¼ teaspoon ground nutmeg
¼ teaspoon ground cardamom
¾ teaspoon salt, plus ½ teaspoon
9 oz (250 g) spiced or ginger cookies
3 tablespoons butter, melted
1 egg white

FILLING

1 cup (250 g) cream cheese, at room temperature
2 tablespoons sugar
4 tablespoons (60 g) butter, melted
2 tablespoons honey or maple syrup to serve

Preheat the oven to 350°F (180°C).

In a large bowl, combine the apple slices, brown and white sugars, cinnamon, nutmeg, cardamom, and ¾ teaspoon of salt and toss together to coat. Leave to stand for 40 minutes, tossing occasionally, until the slices are pliable.

Put the cookies in a food processor and pulse until finely ground. Add the melted butter, the 2 tablespoons of sugar, ½ teaspoon of salt and the egg white and pulse together to combine. Press the mixture into the bottom and sides of a 10 in (25 cm) pie dish.

Bake the tart crust for 10–12 minutes until the edges are slightly brown. Remove from the oven and set aside to cool completely.

In a bowl, combine the cream cheese and sugar and mix until smooth. Spread the mixture on the bottom of the cooled crust.

Drain the apple mixture, discarding any juices. Working from the outside in, arrange the apple slices in a spiral shape until you get to the center. Drizzle the melted butter over the top and bake for 45 minutes or until the apples are tender.

Remove from the oven and set aside to cool for 1 hour before serving, drizzled with honey or maple syrup.

Pairing subtle chai spices with pineapple cream cheese frosting and pineapple flowers makes this cake a winner. The pineapple flowers are best made the day before you need them.

Chai-spiced cake with pineapple frosting

SERVES 8–10

2 chai-flavored tea bags
1½ cups (350 ml) milk
2¼ cups (270 g) all-purpose flour
2 teaspoons baking powder
¾ teaspoon salt
1½ teaspoons ground cinnamon
1 teaspoon ground cardamom
¼ teaspoon ground cloves
1½ teaspoons ground ginger
13 tablespoons (180 g) butter, softened
1 cup (200 g) sugar
½ cup (100 g) light brown sugar
3 large eggs
1 teaspoon vanilla extract

PINEAPPLE FROSTING

1 cup (250 g) cream cheese, at room temperature
2½ sticks (300 g) butter, softened
4 cups (450 g) confectioners' sugar
1 teaspoon vanilla extract
¼ cup (5 g) freeze-dried pineapple, crushed to a powder (optional)

PINEAPPLE FLOWERS
(BEST MADE THE DAY BEFORE)

1 pineapple, peeled and thinly sliced (use a mandoline for best results)

To make the pineapple flowers, preheat the oven to 225°F (100°C) and line 2–3 baking sheets with parchment paper.

Place the pineapple slices onto paper towels to dry, then carefully transfer them to the lined baking sheets. Bake for up to 3 hours, turning the slices over every 30 minutes, until the slices are dry to the touch and slightly golden on the edges. Remove them from the oven and place each slice in the hole of a muffin pan to form cup shapes. Turn the oven off and place the muffin pans back into the still warm oven overnight or 8–10 hours.

Preheat the oven to 350°F (175°C). Grease and flour three 6 in (15 cm) cake pans.

Combine the tea bags and milk in a saucepan and bring to a boil. Remove from the heat and allow to steep for 10–15 minutes. Add extra milk to bring it up to 1 cup (240 ml) if necessary (some milk will have evaporated).

Sift the flour, baking powder, salt and spices into a bowl. Whisk until combined and set aside.

Using a stand mixer or handheld mixer, whisk the butter and sugars at medium speed until pale and fluffy, 3–4 minutes. Reduce the speed and add the eggs, one at a time, making sure each is fully incorporated. Add the vanilla and mix well.
(Recipe continued overleaf)

Using a metal spoon, fold the dry ingredients and the chai milk into the butter mixture, alternating them until all the ingredients are combined.

Transfer the batter to the prepared pans and bake for 35–40 minutes or until a skewer inserted into each cake comes out clean. Remove from the oven and cool in the pans for 15 minutes before turning out to cool completely.

To make the frosting, combine the cream cheese and butter in a stand mixer or bowl and whisk until fluffy, 2–3 minutes. Sift in the confectioners' sugar, one cup at a time, until incorporated, then add the vanilla and the pineapple powder, if using.

To assemble, place one cake layer on a stand or serving plate. Top with some frosting and spread it out evenly. Place a second cake layer on top and again spread it with frosting. Repeat with the third cake. Apply a crumb coat (a thin layer of frosting over the whole cake, which prevents those little stray crumbs getting caught in the main layer) and refrigerate for 20 minutes. Use the remaining frosting to cover the cake. Carefully place the pineapple flowers onto the cake for the final, show-stopping look.

Acknowledgments

There are so many people I would like to thank, whose support, love and never-ending encouragement have helped me through my food writing journey. Publishing my first cookbook was no mean feat, it took me years of hard work and lots of determination, because I had a vision, a dream and a longing to share my story. With so much love and support from so many people it was an amazing success, a beautiful book that is a legacy for my children.

Graham, you have always championed me, always supported me, you are kind-hearted and loving and always encouraging me to achieve my dreams. Our amazing children, Adam and Zara, you both nourish me as a person, and love me as your mother and make me realize every day how lucky I am to have you both in my life.

My parents Hamid and Zarina, without your love and support and video calls every day, I don't think I could have coped being on the other side of the world from you. And Mom, for always showing me that cooking for others is truly an act of love.

My three beautiful sisters, Anjum, Farah and Nishat, your kindness, encouragement and love renews my energy to keep striving to do my best.

I always knew I wanted to write another cookbook, sharing recipes that combine sugar and spice, but also East and West, a perfect blend to take desserts and cakes to another level.

Thank you to the Bateman team for making this vision come to life. Louise Russell, thank you for believing in me right from day one. You gave me the courage to express myself, I love your quiet determination, your knowledge and guidance. Thank you for allowing me to be involved in every aspect of this book. Paul Bateman, thank you for being cake-tester extraordinaire, and for your enthusiasm and support for this book. Renée Lang for your help and support with editing. Sarah Yankelowitz, for your kindness, sensitivity and endless patience while we worked through the design process and all my crazy ideas and endless changes. You have the patience of a saint.

Floor van Lierop, thank you—I know how hard you have worked on this book. Thank you for your enthusiasm and for bringing the design of my vision to life.

Christall Lowe, what a crazy year it was! But we made it, a dream team, and we worked together like a well-oiled machine. From the moment I saw your work, I knew I had to work with you to bring my vision to life. Thank you for bringing such grace, love, light and talent to every photograph. And helping me eat through every cake, dessert and ice cream for breakfast, lunch and dinner on shoot days. And the opera singing, well, every note told me we got the shot we needed. Thank you from the bottom of my heart.

A heart-felt thank you to Al Brown and Peter Gordon, for their kind words and for taking the time to endorse my book. I am truly humbled.

I feel incredibly lucky to have wonderful friends who enrich and support me in so many ways, thank you for always being there, you know who you are.

Finally, thank-you to all my readers and supporters, both in person and online. It is an absolute privilege for me to share my recipes and stories with you, because without you cooking, eating, reading and listening, there is no point in doing what I do. I love being part of a wonderful community that shares my love for food and cooking. I am incredibly grateful to be living in this beautiful country of Aotearoa New Zealand.

Immense gratitude always,

Ashia

Index

D

E

F

G

H

I

R

S

T

U

V

W

Z

First published in 2025 by

Interlink Books
An imprint of Interlink Publishing Group, Inc.
46 Crosby Street
Northampton, Massachusetts 01060
www.interlinkbooks.com

Published simultaneously in New Zealand by
David Bateman Ltd.

www.ashiaismailsinger.com
@myindiankitchenbyashia

Photography: Christall Lowe
Design & typography: Floor van Lierop, thisisthem.com

Library of Congress Cataloging-in-Publication Data available
ISBN 978-1-62371-604-2

Printed and bound in Korea.

Interlink Publishing Group, Inc. is committed to a sustainable future for our business, our readers and our planet. This book is made from Forest Stewardship Council® certified paper.